D0593805

THE INTERFACE BETWEEN PSYCHIATRY
AND ANTHROPOLOGY

The Interface between Psychiatry and Anthropology

By E. D. WITTKOWER and GUY DUBREUIL
ROBERT B. EDGERTON   WALTER GOLDSCHMIDT
LUDWIG VON BERTALANFFY   SEYMOUR S. KETY
G. M. CARSTAIRS

Edited by

IAGO GALDSTON, M.D.

*Chief of Psychiatric Training
Department of Mental Health,
State of Connecticut*

BRUNNER/MAZEL, Publishers • New York
BUTTERWORTHS • London

UNIVERSITY of PENNSYLVANIA
THE ANNENBERG SCHOOL
OF COMMUNICATIONS
PHILADELPHIA, PA. 19104

Library of Congress Catalogue Card No. 77-152687
SBN 87630-035-2

MANUFACTURED IN THE UNITED STATES OF AMERICA

Foreword

The American College of Psychiatrists, since its organization seven years ago, has had as one of its major aims continuing and major academic goals—*"Our college was founded as a forum for the continuing and adjuvant education of its Fellows and Members."* George Gardner said this at the Second Graduate Education Program in New Orleans, January 31, 1969.

The College has been blessed by a remarkable Program Committee under the chairmanship of Iago Galdston. They have brought together, for the past three years, an array of scholars who have added distinction to the academic objectives of this society.

These men have dealt with a host of related topics that test the fundamental principles of psychiatry, psycho-biology, anthropology and sociology—especially appropriate for such a teaching endeavor.

Our thanks to the committee, and to the essayists, with the wish that these writings will bring to our Association added justification for its labors.

FRANK H. LUTON, M.D.
President, 1970

v

American College of Psychiatrists

PRESIDENT 1969
George E. Gardner, M.D.

PROGRAM COMMITTEE 1969

Iago Galdston, M.D.   Robert Jones, M.D.
Norman Brill, M.D.   Albert Silverman, M.D.
Evelyn Ivey, M.D.

PRESIDENT 1970
Frank H. Luton, M.D.

PROGRAM COMMITTEE 1970

Iago Galdston, M.D.   Albert Silverman, M.D.
Norman Brill, M.D.   Henry Brosin, M.D.
Robert Jones, M.D.   Evelyn Ivey, M.D.

Contents

Introduction

The papers in this volume present two unique but related perceptions of one basic issue—that of the interrelationship of anthropology and psychiatry.

In the gross this interrelationship is easily recognized. Anthropology is the study of the extended history of mankind; psychiatry, that of the short-range behavioral history of man. The former is the matrix of the latter and affects it profoundly.

But in the finer respect the interrelationship between psychiatry and anthropology is not widely nor clearly appreciated either among psychiatrists or among anthropologists. The accent here is on *clearly* and *widely,* for it must be acknowledged that in recent decades interest in the interrelationship of psychiatry and anthropology has grown encouragingly.

However there *is* a certain urgency in the pursuit of this study, for psychiatry which has traditionally been parochial in its orientations is now called on to deal with rapidly changing mores and with new areas of concern.

Psychiatry has been for long bound by the so-called normal and by that delineation with the "out of bounds," the abnormal, and the variant. In recent decades, however, the norms of the normal have been questioned and breached.

Minority groups do not accept, nor function by, the criteria of the majority, the statistical normal. Nor do the minority groups share a common set of values, practices or beliefs. The peoples of the third world, the so-called underdeveloped countries, do not appear, as it was believed in the early decades of this century, to adopt the values, norms and living patterns of "the older worlds."

All this is strange and alarming in psychiatry, but in anthropology it has been well known since long ago that the history of mankind has been "polymorphous and mobile." The values, ways and living patterns of different people, living in different parts of the world at the same time and at different times, have differed radically. Psychiatry had largely assumed that there existed a basic prototypical pattern of life for all men. This was a persuasion derived oddly enough both from the Judaic-Christian teachings and from the schema of socio-cultural evolution propounded by the late nineteenth-century evolutionists, notably Herbert Spencer and Auguste Comte.

Anthropology knew much better than psychiatry how much what a man is depends on what he is required to do to subsist. Technology in the basic sense (technology goes way back in the history of man to even before the Eolithic Age) greatly but not entirely shapes man's life. The discovery-invention of agriculture effected the profoundest changes in the patterns of human existence. Most likely it provided the rationale for the patristic family. At the present time we are experiencing most radical technological changes and concomitantly, as well as derivatively, are witnessing very astonishing changes in the mores and values of people, as well as radical changes in the structure and functions of the family.

It is clear that basic assumptions in psychiatry could with much profit be inspected in the perspective of anthropology. Conversely, from psychiatry anthropology can learn much concerning the motives that animate human beings, who though they differ so radically, group from group, share in common some life-essential values and practices. To cite but two, they, in the main, protect their children and they try to treat and cure their sick. As Professor Goldschmidt has shown in his paper, all men esteem excellence (areté) but "the excellence in what" differs radically among different groups.

The two sets of papers in this volume were delivered respectively at the 1969 and the 1970 academic meetings of the American College of Psychiatrists.

The first set of these papers, then, treats of man in global dimensions, the second set in a more restricted range. The first, the terms being allowed, is Macro-anthropology, the second Micro-anthropology. In the latter the focus is not on mankind but on Man—the individual. And the argument advanced is to the effect that the behavioral patterns of man, behavior embracing both the subjective internal and the overtly outward activities of the individual, are conditioned by the three worlds in which man realizes his existence: the world of his subjective immediacies, in the German his *Eigenwelt*—the coexisting intimate world, the *Mitwelt* —and the extending embracing world, the *Umwelt*.

In effect, these are not three separate worlds, but rather three contiguous layers of the unique sphere in which the individual lives and functions.

Psychiatry has been traditionally, that is long before Freud and psychoanalysis came upon the scene, chiefly devoted to, and preoccupied with, man's intrapsychic being and operations.

Only in recent times has the psychiatrist's concern been extended to include the effect on the individual, on his immediate and extended family, of the community in which he dwells and operates, and of the extended world and his position in it. To this extended concern anthropology and sociology have made valuable contributions.

But we are only at the beginning of what may be termed the synergic relations between anthropology and psychiatry (with sociology as a potential third agent). It is to the further advancement of these desirable and necessary developments that the six papers here published are directed.

There remains to be acknowledged, with deep gratitude, the support given these programs by the Geigy Pharmaceuticals Corporation and also the Wenner-Gren Foundation for Anthropological Research. Particular acknowledgement and gratitude is due to Dr. Dita Osmundsen, Director of Research of the Wenner-Gren Foundation, for support and guidance in the formulation of the program on Psychiatry and Anthropology. I am personally grateful to the program committees for their productive participation in the organization of the academic programs of the College.

Finally to the contributors, without whose earnest and generous participation this volume could not be, we are immensely grateful. They were solicited to deal, from the bias of their special interests, with a theme of double polarity—a task calling for vision in depth, and this could well be the subtitle of the texts here published.

IAGO GALDSTON

THE INTERFACE BETWEEN PSYCHIATRY
AND ANTHROPOLOGY

1

Reflections on the Interface between Psychiatry and Anthropology

E. D. WITTKOWER, M.D..
Professor of Psychiatry, McGill University
and
GUY DUBREUIL, Ph.D.
Professeur d'Anthropologie,
Université de Montréal

Psychiatry, according to dictionary definition, is "the medical specialty dealing with mental disorders" whereas anthropology has been defined as "the science of man in relation to physical character, distribution, origin, environmental and social relations, and culture." Both cultural anthropology and psychiatry have in common concern with human behavior. As implied by the definitions given, considerable differences in the orientation of the two disciplines exist. For instance, according to Webster's Dictionary, anthropology is a science and psychiatry is not. The following dissonances between the two disciplines have been identified: (1) Anthropology is a long range study of mankind and psychiatry a short range study of the individual. (2) Anthropology focuses on social structures and culture patterns, psychiatry on individuals. (3) Anthropology concerns

1

itself with the smooth functioning and integration of cultural elements and psychiatry with the psychopathology of the mentally diseased person. (4) Anthropology derived its knowledge of mental disorders, at least in the past, from tribal life, and psychiatry predominantly from Western or Western-type societies, and (5) Anthropology attributes human thought and feelings to a structure which exists in the minds of the adult population at the time of an infant's birth whereas psychoanalytic psychiatry holds that drive energy in the process of the infant's psychosexual development is harnessed by key figures in his environment in accordance with prevailing cultural beliefs, values, customs and practices.

Despite these fundamental differences which have indeed been greatly lessened within recent years, psychiatrists and anthropologists for some time have joined hands and have tried to learn from each other. This rapprochement and interpenetration between the two disciplines is based on both theoretical and practical considerations which after a brief historical introduction will be elaborated in the course of this paper.

A Brief Historical Outline

Emil Kraepelin is usually regarded as one of the earliest pioneers in the comparative study of mental disorders. In 1904 he went to Java with the explicit purpose of finding out whether in this country, as compared with Germany, mental disorders differed in frequency and nature. However, he accounted for the differences which he noted in terms of heredity and race rather than of culture. Roughly about the same time other psychiatrists as well as social scientists, largely anecdotally, reported on such culture-bound syndromes as Amok, Latah and Arctic hysteria (Ellis 1893; Rasch 1894; Van Brero 1895; Metzger 1897; Brill 1913).

Freud early in his career took an interest in cultural

phenomena. He and some of his early followers scanned ethnological literature for confirmation of psychoanalytic theory. In 1918 Freud published *Totem and Taboo* which aroused a good deal of skepticism and indignation (Kroeber 1920) in anthropological circles (La Barre 1958). Nonetheless, in the twenties, leading anthropologists began to recognize the significance of psychological issues in anthropology. In this way the culture and personality movement came into being. Early eminent representatives of this movement who applied psychoanalytic theory to their studies are Edward Sapir (1932, 1934, 1937, 1938, 1939), Ruth Benedict (1934a, 1934b, 1938), and Margaret Mead (1928, 1930, 1934, 1935, 1939, 1940; Mead and Bateson 1942).

Interest in psychiatry by anthropologists was reciprocated by psychiatrists. Consequently previous to the Second World War research teams composed of psychiatrists and anthropologists were formed in increasing numbers. Well-known are the researches and publications by Mekeel (1943), Kardiner, Linton, DuBois, and West (1945), Leighton and Kluckhohn (1947), Róheim (1950), and Devereux (1961a, 1961b).

This spirit of cooperation between the two disciplines has been maintained during the post war years despite dissenting voices; it has increased considerably during recent years. This recent increase of interest in each other's discipline may be due (a) to a shift of scientific curiosity on the part of anthropologists from a sole concern with sociocultural institutions to an interest in motivation and meaning of human behavior, (b) to the ease of travel, combined with an awareness of the interdependence of the world in the nuclear age which brought psychiatrists face to face with psychological problems in other countries, (c) to a creation of a new brand of psychiatrist whose perspective is not confined to the boundaries of the mental hospital grounds or the four walls of his office, and (d) as far as therapeutic considerations are concerned, to a growing sense of social responsibility which gave rise to the present popularity of social psychiatry. One branch of this wide and hybrid field is cultural psychiatry; its extension beyond the boundaries of one culture is transcultural psychiatry.

Scientific contributions to this field have been made, alone or as team members, by cultural anthropologists, psychoanalysts, psychiatrists, sociologists, social psychologists, communication theorists, epidemiologists, social workers and economists. Some of them have had training in more than one of these disciplines. Originally foreign nationals, mostly Americans, predominated among research workers in developing countries. Of late, with the conquest of infectious diseases and a perceptible increase in trained psychiatrists in these countries, indigenous psychiatrists have gratifyingly taken an ever-increasing part in the study of cultural psychiatric problems in their countries.

Objectives

What then can representatives of the two disciplines gain by cooperation with each other? In brief, acquisition of skills, such as interviewing techniques and research designs, deepening and widening of understanding, i.e. conceptual crossfertilization, and as far as mental illness is concerned, improvement in the care of the mentally ill and potential reduction of the frequency of its occurrence. Research collaboration between anthropologists and psychiatrists is by no means easy. It requires tolerance for different viewpoints and approaches, tact with regard to status differences, translation of idioms, bridging of concepts, and dovetailing data obtained by different methodologies.

More specifically the following areas of mutual concern to both disciplines can be identified: (1) Personality structure in relation to different patterns of child-rearing and different social sanctions in different cultures; (2) Crosscultural differences in unconsciously preferred ego defense mechanisms; (3) The range of normal and abnormal behavior, feelings and thoughts in different cultures; (4) Sociocultural factors predisposing to mental health or to optimal function; (5) Sociocultural factors predisposing to mental ill health; (6) Crosscultural differences in the frequency and distribution of mental disorders; (7) Crosscultural differences in the form, course and manifestation of mental illness; (8) The forms of treatment practiced or preferred in various sociocultural settings; (9) Beliefs regarding the causation of behavioral deviance and mental illness; (10) Differences in the attitudes towards the mentally ill in different cultures, and (11) Planned sociocultural changes conducive to prevention of mental ill health.

A few examples illustrative of the items listed must suffice.

Theory

As stated before, psychiatry and especially psychoanalysis have had a profound effect on anthropological theory.

Many convergent factors could explain this influence. For a long time, anthropologists have been unaware of this convergence. The first anthropological assumption, made by some 19th-century Occidental thinkers, was that strange exotic customs, queer prehistoric remains, odd linguistic forms and racial traits could be explained only through their inclusion in a long range evolutionary vista. Later, under the influence of Emile Durkheim, a new assumption was added, to wit, social phenomena could be explained only by reference to other social phenomena. Consequently, one of the strongest pleas of Durkheim and his followers was against psychological interpretations of social facts. Durkheim stated: "Whenever a social phenomenon is directly explained by a psychological phenomenon, we may be sure that the explanation is false" (1901 p. 128). Such statements became dogmas in many anthropological circles. For instance, the English School of Social Anthropology endeavored to show, sometimes with great sophistication, how most social customs could be explained in terms of social structures and functions. Some anthropologists, especially Claude Lévi-Strauss, argued that most social rules, running from incest taboos to such brittle habits as cigarette and Christmas gift exchanges, stem from the need of all societies (and perhaps of all human beings) to organize systematic networks of exchange based on coherent social reciprocity (1949). More recently, some anthropologists have been studying different aspects of culture, such as mythology, in order to arrive at hidden basic structures of meanings (Lévi-Strauss 1962a, 1962b, 1964, 1966; Turner 1967). In the United States, similar trends have prevailed but with a greater emphasis on diachronic considerations, culture patterns and culture change (Lowie 1937).

All these studies—and many more examples could be added—presuppose hidden structures, principles or symbolic elements. At their own level, many of them are fully satisfactory and psychological factors would add nothing essential to them. However, they raise one capital issue: if these principles or elements are operative in human groups, they must be congruous with the human psyche. Furthermore, if they are not known to the actors themselves, they must be based on unconscious psychological mechanisms which can only be found in individuals.

Here lies the basic junction between anthropology and psychiatry. "The true locus of culture," wrote Sapir, "is in the interactions of specific individuals and, on the subjective side, in the world of meanings which each one of these individuals may unconsciously abstract for himself from his participation in these interactions" (1932).

Prior to Sapir, the prevailing tendency among anthropologists was to reject, ignore or belittle the value of Freudian ideas for the interpretation of universal psychological processes (Kluckhohn 1944; La Barre 1958). Illustrative of this attitude is Malinowski's well-known refutation of the universality of the Oedipus complex (1925, 1926, 1927). Nevertheless, Malinowski's theses, along with a few others (Rivers 1926; Seligman 1924, 1929), relied partly upon some of the most fundamental psychoanalytical assumptions regarding psychic structure and basic mechanisms of defense and adjustment. Moreover, in opposition to most ethnographic monographs, references to individuals were abundant in their works and deviants were sometimes alluded to. These anthropological essays, together with Sapir's articles on culture and the individual, had two major effects: they sharpened some psychiatrists' views on the degree of variability of "human nature" and they awakened some anthropologists to the possibility of knowing more about culture through the individual.

Whereas this widening of the anthropological perspective prompted psychoanalysts to conduct anthropological field research, it also prompted some anthropologists to borrow or devise field work techniques which would enable them both to study the individual in his culture and to take into account some psychiatric propositions.

The first of these techniques was collection of life histories in the field. The most enduring influence on the sophisticated use of the life history method was made by Paul Radin (1913, 1920) when he published his two versions of the autobiography of a Winnebago Indian. This technique was later systematically described by some anthropologists such as Dollard (1935), Kluckhohn (1945) and Langness (1965) and is now well accepted in anthropology. A recent extension of the life history method is the "family autobiography" which sometimes gives a vivid picture of family dynamics besides giving precious insights into how the individual experiences his culture (Lewis 1959, 1961, 1964; Mintz 1960).

Projective techniques were also used in the field after the pioneer works of Hallowell (1941a, 1941b, 1942, 1945,

1951), Jules Henry (1941) and William E. Henry (1947).
Drawing analysis was added to some anthropologists' techniques (Anastasi and Foley 1938; Belo 1955; Dennis 1960;
Dubois 1944; Haddon 1904; Honigmann and Carrera 1957;
Schubert 1930), while others collected dreams, visions and
phantasies (Barnouw 1949; D'Andrade 1961; Eggan 1949,
1952, 1955, 1961; Field 1960; Seligman 1924). Art and folklore also came to be described and analyzed in the light of
psychoanalytic concepts (McClelland and Friedman 1952;
Heyer 1953; La Barre 1961; Lantis 1953; Wright 1954).

The inclusion of the individual within the anthropological vista also prompted more and more anthropologists to
test psychiatric concepts in the field, as Opler (1936a,
1936b, 1938) did among the Apache and Hallowell (1938a,
1938b, 1939, 1940) among the Saulteaux, and to investigate
more and more deeply such problems as childhood determinism, psychological mechanisms underlying witchcraft,
learning processes, normality versus abnormality, delinquency and marginality, and mental disease.

Finally one should mention the crosscultural research
initiated at Yale which is partly devoted to testing some
psychiatric hypotheses, such as relating types of infantile
experience to some cultural elements (Whiting and Child
1953; Whiting 1959, 1961).

On the whole, these studies have tended to show to the
anthropologists that, as Hartmann, Kris and Loewenstein
put it: "No short-cuts from institutionalized behavior to an
individual attitude or tendency are psychologically war-
ranted" (1951 p. 28).

Conversely, psychiatry has learned a great deal from
anthropology regarding the etiology, symptomatology, treatment, and prevention of mental disorders.

Etiology

Anthropologists have always insisted on the use of a
relativistic yardstick in measuring normal and abnormal be-

havior. Nevertheless, a growing number of evidences indicates that mental illness is found in all human societies (Benedict and Jacks 1954; Leighton and Hughes 1961; Wittkower et al. 1960; Murphy 1962; Murphy et al. 1967). On the other hand, no culture studied by psychologically minded anthropologists with or without the cooperation of psychiatrists has failed to reveal some sources of stress. Indeed the cultural stresses in some of the so-called primitive societies have been found to be quite considerable. These facts tend to indicate that culture *per se*, envisioned as a mould imposed upon human drives and as a constellation of stimuli for human thought, sentiment and behavior, universally generates psychological and even biological tensions which are liable to be experienced as stressful by individuals. Everywhere, some of them become mentally ill, whereas others become deviants, delinquents or reformers.

Cultural stress factors known to have a harmful effect on mental health fall into three broad categories: cultural content, social organization and sociocultural change. Cultural content refers to all beliefs, values, norms, attitudes and customs contained in a people's culture. Social organization is the network of regular and relatively long-standing interactions between individuals and between groups of individuals, within a society. Sociocultural change means any modification undergone in the cultural content and in the social organization.

Cultural Content

Basically, the relationship between cultural content and mental diseases is the degree of psychological tension and anxiety which can be created by some cultural elements between individuals and within individuals. The following cultural elements seem to be among the major sources of stress.

(a) *Taboos.* Excessive taboos imposed by a culture upon a population or upon certain social groups, such as prohibitions placed upon women in some North African societies (Lewin 1958), may deprive certain individuals of basic gratifications.

(b) *Value saturation.* While most individuals are reasonably guided in their thought, attitudes and behavior by cultural goals and values, some individuals become so imbued with them that it amounts almost to an intoxication. This phenomenon may be called value saturation. In most cases of value saturation, it is not easy to discern the normal from the abnormal. For instance, Wallace (1959) cites the case of Aharihon, an Onondoga war captive who was the idol of Iroquois youth because they could recognize in him the ego ideal established by their culture. However, Aharihon had lived to such an extreme the Iroquis model of manhood, especially the virtues of bravery and cruelty in war, that he also could have been considered a killer. Similar cases occurred in Germany before and during the last world war. It would seem that some cultural and social situations predispose to value saturation.

(c) *Value polymorphism.* This expression refers to the coexistence within the same cultural system or within the same individual of values that are antagonistic. There are three major aspects of value polymorphism: (1) The first aspect is cultural pluralism by which, especially in complex societies, an individual is confronted with different ideologies, moral norms and religious dogmas; (2) Value polymorphism can also be related to cultural discontinuity (Benedict 1949) and to role replacement (Wallace 1961 p. 186). For instance, when a culture does not provide proper and clear strategies such as "rites de passage" for important changes in the individual's life cycle, or when the transitions and the roles themselves are ambiguously defined, the individuals may find themselves confronted with contradictory values and behavioral norms, unable to choose which could introduce them to their future status. The passage from adolescence to adulthood in Occidental cultures is a pertinent example;

(3) The last aspect of value polymorphism is the excessive exposure of individuals to simultaneous status. For instance, the status of executive in business may burden some individuals with so much responsibility that performance of their work interferes with duties and gratifications derived from such other status as father, husband and friend.

(d) *Culture-bound systems of sentiments.* In some African cultures, fear of black magic and of evil spirits is so universal and so pronounced that everybody is suspicious of everybody (Field 1960). Among the Aborigines of New Guinea, "both fear and aggression are deliberately fostered" (Berndt 1962 p. 405). There is good reason to believe that such culture-bound sentiments make some individuals particularly prone to mental illness.

(e) *Basic personality structure and child training.* Both these factors may predispose to mental illness in many different ways. For instance, in some Senegalese cultures, children are trained in such a manner that their ego remains weak when they reach adulthood (Collomb 1967). This seems to explain why members of such African societies easily "go to pieces" if subjected to relatively minor stressful situations. The fragile personality of the Alorese has been attributed to inconsistent child training (Dubois 1944), and the schizoid characteristics of the Balinese to the withdrawal of affection by the mother experienced in childhood (Mead and MacGregor 1951).

Social Organization

Three aspects of social organization relating to mental illness deserve special attention: anomie, social rigidity and minority status.

(a) *Anomie.* The general relationship between anomie (normlessness or fragility of norms) and increased frequency of mental illness and delinquency has been established for a relatively long time (Durkheim 1893; Faris and Dunham

1938; Merton 1938; Faris 1944; Cohen 1955, 1959). However, this relationship involves many different and complex factors, such as low standards of education, poverty, migration, ethnic diversity, high demographic concentration, and movement of mentally ill persons into slum areas. A common feature which underlies the interplay of these factors seems to be the loss of meaning of cultural norms and values.

(b) *Social rigidity.* It is almost impossible to measure the over-all rigidity of a social system. However, it would seem that, in small communities dominated by isolation, by strict traditional values and by a social structure which imposes on individuals specific status and roles, individuals unable to knuckle down to passive conformism feel so constrained that intense emotional tension ensues (Bastide 1965).

(c) *Minority status.* Cultural, social or racial groups become vulnerable to mental disease when they are or feel reduced to an inferior status. It has been suggested that many members of such groups suffer from a complex of depersonalization or alienation, which undermines and confuses their ego identity. The case of American Negroes is well known in that respect (Kardiner and Ovesey 1951). According to A. F. C. Wallace (1961, p. 145), the Seneca Indians became quasi-pathological when they realized their socioeconomic situation and the very poor opinion held by the whites regarding their language and culture. Similar reactions occurred among the Aborigines of New Guinea (Burton-Bradley 1968). Nativistic or revivalist movements often result from such minority situations, such as the Cargo Cult (also called Vailala Madness) of New Guinea (Berndt 1952-53, 1954; Brown 1966; Lawrence 1964; Schwartz 1962). Examples of similar movements are numerous and well documented (Lanternari 1963). Whereas some of these movements may have positive functions, such as certain revitalization processes mentioned by Wallace (1956), many seem to be collective afflictions leading to dysfunctional beliefs, sentiments and behavior.

Sociocultural Change

Sociocultural change does not necessarily produce adverse emotional reaction and social disorganization. For instance, the Kamba, a Bantu tribe of Africa, seem to adapt easily to various new situations because of the high degree of individualism and structural "looseness" of their culture (Oliver 1965). Yet, it has also been demonstrated that some types of sociocultural change can be noxious. For instance, Hallowell's study of the Ojibwa (1955) clearly indicates that those Ojibwa who were partly acculturated had a "regressive" personality. Obviously such negative psychological effects are not due exclusively to cultural change. Other factors such as minority situation, low social status, poverty, types of contacts with the dominant group and the speed of acculturation, are also at work. Factors involved in such situations are so numerous and intricately related to each other that it is very difficult to pinpoint the specific effect of each (Murphy 1961). On the whole, it would seem that their influence varies in function of their interrelatedness in different sociocultural situations. As Talcott Parsons puts it, "A society in which there is a good deal of 'disorganization' and 'pathology' is almost certainly the necessary price of dynamic openness to progressive change" (1951a, p. 309).

Symptomatology

There is general agreement that symptomatological similarities rather than dissimilarities prevail in a global view of *schizophrenia*. The clinical subforms of schizophrenia (simple, hebephrenic, catatonic, paranoid) occur everywhere though in varying frequencies. The alleged rarity of schizophrenia simplex in some societies may be due to acceptance of low work performance by the community. If everybody is idle, to be idle on pathological grounds is nothing exceptional. Catatonic states are by no means pathognomonic for schizophrenia in some developing countries. They occur as brief psychogenic episodes and are related in their frequency to the tendency of native populations to regress massively in response to stress. While chronic schizophrenic catatonic states have become rare in Europe and America, they are common in India and other Asiatic countries. The frequency of catatonic stupors in these countries may be due to the teaching both by Hinduism and Buddhism of social and emotional withdrawal as an acceptable mode of reacting to difficulties, and the frequency of catatonic rigidity and of negativism in Indian schizophrenics, to a traditional passive-aggressive response to a threatening world. By contrast, the maintenance of social contacts in Southern Italian schizophrenics, even in advanced stages, has been attributed to their traditional sociability and to their great family solidarity (Parsons 1961). Observers from both Africa and India agree that paranoid formations in schizophrenic patients under their care are less systematized than in Euro-Americans (Hoch 1959, 1961). The paucity of delusional content in these patients may be due to their lack of education. It is obvious that varying cultural beliefs mould the content of delusions and hallucinations. For instance an Eskimo who has not learned about the existence of Jesus Christ or General de Gaulle can obviously not imagine that he is either of them in his grandiose psychotic ideas, just as in the African bush an indigenous paranoid patient will accuse a sorcerer of bewitching him and will feel persecuted by spirits rather than by X-rays, radio, or television. An Austrian psychiatrist (Lenz 1964) studied changes in schizophrenic symptomatology during the last hundred years. On comparison of the first fifty years period with the second fifty years period he found that the ideas of being persecuted by God or devil have become infrequent and ideas of being persecuted by material agents more common. According to Japanese investigators (Hasuzawa 1963; Asai 1964), paranoid schizophrenia has increased in Japan since the Second World War. Since then, in replacement of delusions regarding the Emperor, paranoid delusions have concerned themselves increasingly with the United States, the Communist Party, radio, and television.

The typical symptoms of *endogenous depression*, according to our observations, are most commonly found among Europeans irrespective of where they live (Murphy et al. 1967). Atypical features have been noted in others (Van Wulfften-Palthe 1936, Oesterreicher 1950, Pfeiffer 1969). Outstanding among these are the frequency of hypochondriacal ideas, the frequency of persecutory ideas and the rarity or absence of feelings of unworthiness, of guilt, and of having sinned in some cultural areas. Feelings of unworthiness and of guilt in depressives are most pronounced in Euro-Americans (Murphy et al. 1967); they are infrequent in Japanese, Chinese, Indians, Pakistanis and Arabs. They are notably rare in Africans south of the Sahara. Content-wise, self-accusatory ideas may be concerned with trespasses on morality, on society or on worship of ancestors or deities. Guilt feelings in depressives are absent in societies in which superego pressures are externalized, and feelings of having sinned can be experienced only if the concept of sin is accepted by one's religious belief system. Projection of id impulses and of superego censures onto the outer world, so common in developing countries, counteracts feelings of guilt but results in paranoid formations which may obscure the depressive picture. As regards hypochondriacal sensations, incapacity to give verbal expression to feelings may account for their frequency in depressed preliterates. It is also possible, as Collomb and Zwingelstein (1961) have suggested for the Senegalese, that continuous skin contact between mother and child reinforces libidinization of the body and therefore predisposes to pathological body sensations in depressives.

There is a group of mental disorders which have been

labeled *culture-bound reactive syndromes*. Strictly speaking they are not culture-bound. It would be more appropriate to speak of culture specific variants of psychological reactions or mental disorders also known to occur elsewhere.

Yap (1969) has divided them into primary fear reactions, such as the Latah reaction, hyperidic rage reactions such as Amok, culturally imposed nosophobias, such as Koro, and dissociation, such as trance and possession states.

These disorders have been subjected to and indeed require combined pychiatric-anthropological understanding and interpretation.

A typical example is Koro, a disorder which has been reported from Southeast Asia (Van Wulfften-Palthe 1936). Attributed by its sufferers to sexual excesses and masturbation it is a state of anxiety amounting to a panic lest the penis may shrink and retract into the abdomen. Efforts are made by the patient and his family to forestall such a calamity by pulling the penis out and fixing it to a wooden box. Phenomenologically Koro resembles in many respects castration anxiety so common in Euro-Americans (Rin 1963). But it differs in the way in which the threat to the genitals is experienced—as a fear of the penis retracting into the abdomen—and in the manner in which the irrational fear is dealt with, namely by pulling the penis out and fixing it to a box. Psychodynamically, the presenting symptom is probably based on an unresolved Oedipal conflict, but it is also deeply rooted in fundamental Chinese concepts of sexuality. Moreover, it has been suggested that the susceptibility of the Chinese to symbolic castration threats may be related to their oral orientation and to fear of oral deprivation (Weakland 1956).

Treatment

In many developing countries the care of the mentally ill is predominantly in the hands of native healers. They fall into two categories: herbalists and religious healers. The treatment procedure adopted by religious healers is based on animistic beliefs and is symbolic and magical in nature.

Factors which have been identified as operative in these procedures are: (1) the usage of potent drugs such as Rauwolfia and of placebos; (2) rationalization of fears of unknown origin, for example, "Sopono, the Smallpox god, has inflicted this on you;" (3) suggestion reinforced by the high prestige of the native healer resulting in repression; (4) projection of internal badness onto vicious deities; (5) displacement of internal badness on a scapegoat or any other sacrificial animal; (6) displacement of target of attack, that is, the killing of an animal in lieu of a person; (7) penance by sacrifice of considerable monetary value, and (8) group ego support by joining religious cults.

It should be realized that procedures adopted by native healers in the milieu in which they operate are often more effective than so-called scientific procedures; that scientific procedures, such as the E.C.T. machine, may be interpreted by the native population as magic; that Westernization is often skin deep and that not infrequently even after successful treatment at a Western-type hospital a patient is likely to return to the native healer to have "the real cause" of the illness dealt with. In accordance with these cultural considerations, Western-type mental health services cannot be transplanted to developing countries without culturally adapted modifications. Lambo (1956) for instance recognized a long time ago that his Yoruba patients in Nigeria are averse to being admitted to a hospital. He therefore set up village settlements in the vicinity of the mental hospital where patients live with their relatives who prepare their food and give them nursing care.

Culture-determined preferences for forms of treatment exist. Accordingly it is hardly surprising that preference is given: in Germany to autogenic training, a kind of self-imposed drill affecting thought, feeling and behavior, in

Japan to Morita therapy, an ego-directed selfcontrolling procedure based on Zen Buddhism, and in Soviet Russia to collective procedures aimed at restoration of the capacity to work. Contrary to common belief psychoanalysis never gained ground in Austria and in Germany. A prerequisite for its acceptance is a predilection or at least tolerance for individualism which is said to be an American characteristic.

As regards America, ethnic differences in the response to psychotherapy have been noted. J. Spiegel (1959), in a classic study, dealt with the cultural aspects of transference and countertransference phenomena as they occur in psychotherapy. On the strength of observations made on comparison of urban middle class Americans with working class Irish-Americans he argues that transference and countertransference phenomena, from the cultural point of view, represent resistances against dominant middle class values. He suggests that psychotherapeutic procedures be modified in accordance with value orientations prevailing in ethnic groups, such as Irish-Americans.

Prevention

Another recent development has been the application of anthropological knowledge to medicine, not only in exotic cultures, but also in industrialized societies.

However, problems of prevention have not yet been tackled with satisfactory results. In the past and even today as noted by Margaret Mead (1952), the moralistic tendency of anthropologists and psychiatrists has blurred their objectivity in that respect. From this point of view, prevention was too often limited to diatribes against institutions deemed as damaging as well as against child-raising techniques considered as ill-adapted to children's needs. This, of course, was unrealistic and dangerous.

It is true that some changes, such as self-demand feeding, have been induced by the diffusion of some psychiatric creeds. The break-down of tradition, coupled with the anxieties produced by migrations, rapid social changes and many other factors, has obviously made more and more people search for guidance by different specialists. This very fact, besides the dramatic need for prevention, raises profound ethical and ideological problems. For, in the field of human engineering, who can be sure that the induced changes will be beneficial and will not provoke new disequilibria? Furthermore, to what degree should ideological passions and pressures be accepted by acting anthropologists and psychiatrists?

Nevertheless the problem of prevention cannot be avoided. All cultures intentionally or unintentionally take measures to forestall mental illness. For instance, all cultures provide for "cathartic strategies," to use Wallace's expression (Wallace 1961, p. 190), such as periodic carnivals, feasts, games where diverse techniques, like intoxication, torture, dance or trance, are permitted. Status reversal rituals, by which the rich and powerful are humiliated by the poor and humble, are in many cultures what Victor Turner (1969, p. 185) describes as "devices that cleanse society of its structurally engendered 'sins' and what hippies might call 'hang-ups.'" With many other devices, such strategies seem to alleviate psychological tensions arising from taboos, social inequalities and other social imperfections.

On the other hand, inhibition of these cultural strategies for the sake of the highly valued social conformity, especially in North America, may have reduced the beneficial effects of these institutionalized emotional outlets. Consequently we witness nowadays the germination of such patterned strategies as organized gangs, religious and political sects, youth carnivals, hippy communities, and psychotherapeutic groups. Such movements could very well be intrinsically similar to so-called primitive customs previously mentioned and could be considered as having positive functions. Parsons (1951b) has suggested that the increase in chronic mental illness could be related to the American reluctance to accept deviancy. If this were so, the American society, like any other society, would have the choice between different forms of deviancy and cultural strategies, among which mental disease is but one part.

Instead of limiting prevention to often desultory advice against traditional institutions and values, it would seem that efforts should be made to encompass all its implications with all pertinent psychocultural factors. Here, anthropology, with its keener view of significant culture processes, can furnish a most precious contribution.

In the preceding an outline of the borderline area between psychiatry and cultural anthropology has been presented. Inevitably in such an outline it is not possible to name all those who have made valuable contributions to this field of research and practice. As stated in its title the aim of this paper has been to present "Some Reflections on the Interface between Psychiatry and Anthropology."

REFERENCES

ANASTASI, A., and FOLEY, J. P. 1938. A study of animal drawings by Indian children of the North Pacific Coast. *J. Soc. Psychol.*, 9: 363-374.

ASAI, T. 1964. The contents of delusions of schizophrenic patients in Japan: Comparison between periods 1941-1961. *Transcultural Psychiatric Research Review*, 1: 27-28.

BARNOUW, V. 1949. The phantasy world of a Chippewa woman. *Psychiatry*, 12: 67-76.

BASTIDE, R. 1965. *Sociologie des maladies mentales.* Paris: Flammarion. Pp. 106-112.

BELO, J. 1955. Balinese children's drawings. In M. Mead and M. Wolfenstein (Eds.), *Childhood in contemporary cultures.* Chicago: University of Chicago Press. Pp. 52-67.

BENEDICT, P. K., and JACKS, I. 1954. Mental illness in primitive societies. *Psychiatry*, 17: 377-389.

BENEDICT, R. F. 1934a. *Patterns of culture.* Boston: Houghton, Mifflin.

BENEDICT, R. F. 1934b. Anthropology and the abnormal. *J. Gen. Psychol.*, 10: 59-80.

BENEDICT, R. F. 1938. Continuities and discontinuities in cultural conditioning. *Psychiatry*, 1: 161-167.

BENEDICT, R. F. 1949. Continuities and discontinuities in cultural conditioning. In C. Kluckhohn and H. A. Murray (Eds.), *Personality in nature, society and culture.* New York: Alfred A. Knopf. Pp. 414-423.

BERNDT, R. M. 1952-1953. A cargo movement in the eastern central highlands of New Guinea. *Oceania, 23:* 40-69, 137-158, 202-234.

BERNDT, R. M. 1954. Reaction to contact in the eastern highlands of New Guinea. *Oceania.* 24: 191-228, 255-274.

BERNDT, R. M. 1962. *Excess and restraint: Social control among the New Guinea Mountain People.* Chicago: University of Chicago Press.

BRILL, A. 1913. Piblokto or hysteria among Peary's Eskimo. *Journal of Nervous and Mental Diseases.* 40: 514-520.

BROWN, P. 1966. Social change and social movements. In E. K. Fisk (Ed.), *New Guinea on the threshold,* Canberra: Australian National University Press. Pp. 149-166.

BURTON-BRADLEY, B. 1968. Mixed-race society in Port Moresby. *New Guinea Research Bulletin,* No. 23, Australian National University, Canberra.

COHEN, A. K. 1955. *Delinquent boys: The culture of the gang.* New York: Free Press.

COHEN, A. K. 1959. The study of social disorganization and deviant behavior. In R. K. Merton, L. Broom, and L. S. Cottrell, Jr. (Eds.), *Sociology today: Problems and prospects.* New York: Basic Books.

COLLOMB, H. 1967. La position du conflit et les structures familiales en voie de transformation. *Can. Psychiat. Assoc. J.,* 12: 451-465.

COLLOMB, H., and ZWINGELSTEIN, J. 1961. Depressive states in an African community. First Pan African Psychiatric Conference Government Pointer, Ibadan.

D'ANDRADE, R. G. 1961. Anthropological study of dreams. In F. L. K. Hsu (Ed.), *Psychological anthropology.* Homewood, Illinois: Dorsey Press, Pp. 296-332.

DENNIS, W. 1960. The human figure drawings of Bedouins. *Journal of Social Psychology,* 52: 209-219.

DEVEREUX, G. 1961a. *Mohave ethnopsychiatry and suicide: The psychiatric knowledge and the psychic disturbances of an Indian tribe.* Washington, D. C.: United States Government Printing Office.

DEVEREUX, G. 1961b. Two types of model personality models. In B. Kaplan (Ed.), *Studying personality cross-culturally.* New York: Harper and Row.

DOLLARD, J. 1935. *Criteria for the life history.* New Haven, Connecticut: Yale University Press.

DUBOIS, C. 1944. *The people of Alor.* Minneapolis: University of Minnesota Press.

DURKHEIM, E. 1893. *Le suicide. Etude de sociologie.* Paris: Félix Alcan.

DURKHEIM, E. 1901. *Les règles de la méthode sociologique.* (2nd ed.) Paris: Félix Alcan.

EGGAN, D. 1949. The significance of dreams for anthropological research. *American Anthropologist,* 51: 177-198.

EGGAN, D. 1952. The manifest content of dreams: a challenge to social science. *American Anthropologist.* 54: 469-485.

EGGAN, D. 1955. The personal use of myth in dreams. *Journal of American Folklore*, 68: 67-75.

EGGAN, D. 1961. Dream analysis. In B. Kaplan (Ed.), *Studying personality cross-culturally*. New York: Harper and Row. Pp. 567-568.

ELLIS, W. G. 1893. The Amok of the Malays. *Journal of Mental Science*. 39: 325-338.

FARIS, E. L., and DUNHAM, H. W. 1938. *Mental disorders in urban areas*. New York: Rinehart.

FARIS, R. E. L. 1944. Ecological factors in human behavior. In J. McV. Hunt (Ed.), *Personality and the behavior disorders*. Vol. II. New York: The Ronald Press. Pp. 736-757.

FIELD, M. J. 1960. Search for security. *An ethno-psychiatric study of rural Ghana*. Evanston, Illinois: Northwestern University Press.

FREUD, S. 1918. *Totem and Taboo*. New York: Moffat, Yard.

FREUD, S. 1930. *Civilization and its discontents*. New York: Norton.

HADDON, A. C. 1904. Drawings of natives of British New Guinea. *Man*, 4: 33-36.

HALLOWELL, A. I. 1938a. Fear and anxiety as cultural and individual variables in a primitive society. *Journal of Abnormal and Social Psychology*, 33: 25-49.

HALLOWELL, A. I. 1938b. Shabwan. *American Journal of Orthopsychiatry*, 7: 329-340.

HALLOWELL, A. I. 1939. Sin, sex and sickness in Saulteaux belief. *British Journal of Medical Psychology*, 8: 191-197.

HALLOWELL, A. I. 1940. Aggression in Saulteaux society. *Psychiatry*. 3: 395-407.

HALLOWELL, A. I. 1941a. The Rorschach method as an aid in the study of personalities in primitive societies. *Character and Personality*, 9: 235-245.

HALLOWELL, A. I. 1941b. The Rorschach test as a tool for investigating cultural variables and individual differences in the study of personality in primitive societies. *Rorschach Research Exchange*, 5: 31-34

HALLOWELL, A. I. 1942. Acculturation processes and personality changes as indicated by the Rorschach technique. *Rorschach Research Exchange*, 6: 42-50.

HALLOWELL, A. I. 1945. Popular responses and cultural differences: An analysis based on frequencies in a group of American Indian subjects. *Rorschach Research Exchange*, 9: 153-68.

HALLOWELL, A. I. 1951. The use of projective techniques and the study of sociopsychological aspects of aculturation. *Journal of Projective Techniques*, 15: 27-44.

HALLOWELL, A. I. 1955. *Culture and experience*. Philadelphia: University of Pennsylvania Press.

HARTMANN, H., KRIS, E., and LOEWENSTEIN, R. M. 1951. Some psychoanalytic comments on 'culture and personality.' In G. B. Wilbur and W. Muensterberger (Eds.), *Psychoanalysis and culture*. New York: International Universities Press, Inc.

HASUZAWA, T. 1963. Chronological observations of delusions in schizophrenics. In H. Akimoto (Ed.), *Proceedings of the Joint Meeting of the
Japanese Society of Psychiatry and Neurology and the American
Psychiatric Association, Tokyo.* Supplement No. 7 of *Folia Psychiatria
et Neurologia Japonica.*

HENRY, J. 1941. Rorschach technique in primitive culture. *American Journal of Orthopsychiatry.* 11: 230-234.

HENRY, W. E. 1947. The thematic apperception technique in the study of
culture-personality relations. *Genetic Psychology Monograph.* 35: 3-135.

HEYER, V. 1953. Relations between men and women in Chinese stories. In
M. Mead and R. Metraux (Eds.), *The study of culture at a distance.*
Chicago: University of Chicago Press. Pp. 221-234.

HOCH, E. M. 1959. Psychiatrische Beobachtungen und Erfahrungen an
Indischen Patienten. *Praxis (Bern),* 48: 1051-1057.

HOCH, E. M. 1961. Letter. In *Transcultural Psychiatric Research Review,*
No. 11: 65-71.

HONIGMANN, J. J. and CARRERA, R. N. 1957. Cross-cultural use of Mach-
over's Figure Drawing Test. *American Anthropologist.* 59: 650-654.

HUGHES, C., TREMBLY, M. A., RAPOPORT, R. N. and LEIGHTON, A. H. 1960.
People of cove and woodlot: Communities from the viewpoint of social
psychiatry. New York: Basic Books.

KARDINER, A. (in collaboration with LINTON, R., DUBOIS, C., and WEST, J.).
1945. *The psychological frontiers of society.* New York: Columbia
University.

KARDINER, A., and OVESEY, L. 1951. *The mark of oppression.* New York:
Norton.

KLUCKHOHN, C. 1944. The influence of psychiatry on anthropology in
America during the past one hundred years. In J. K. Hall, G. Zil-
boorg, and H. A. Bunker (Eds.), *One hundred years of American
psychiatry.* New York: Columbia University Press. Pp. 589-617.

KLUCKHOHN, C. 1945. The personal document in anthropological science.
In L. Gottschalk, C. Kluckhohn, and R. Angell (Eds.), *The use of
personal documents in history, anthropology, and sociology.* New York:
Social Science Research Council. 53: 79-173.

KRAEPELIN, E. 1904. Vergleichende Psychiatrie. *Zentralblatt fuer Nerven-
heilkunde und Psychiatrie,* 27: 433-437

KROEBER, A. L. 1920. Totem and taboo: An ethnologic psychoanalysis.
American Anthropologist, 22: 48-55.

LA BARRE: W. 1958. The influence of Freud on anthropology. *The American Imago,* 15: 275-328.

LABARRE, W. 1961. Art and mythology. In B. Kaplan (Ed.), *Studying
personality cross-culturally.* New York: Harper and Row. Pp. 394-403.

LAMBO, T. A. 1956. Neuropsychiatric observations in the western region of
Nigeria. *British Medical Journal,* 2: 1388.

LANGNESS, L. L. 1965. *The life history in anthropological science.* New
York: Holt, Rinehart and Winston.

LANTERNARI, W. 1963. *The religions of the oppressed.* New York: Alfred
A. Knopf.

LANTIS, M. 1953. Nunivah Eskimo personality as revealed in the mythology. *Anthropological Papers of the University of Alaska*, 2: 109-174.
LAWRENCE, P. 1964. *Road belong cargo*. Manchester: The University Press.
LEIGHTON, A. H., and HUGHES, J. M. 1961. Cultures as causative of mental disorder. *The Milbank Memorial Fund Quarterly*. 39: 446-448.
LEIGHTON, D. C., and KLUCKHOHN, C. 1947. *Children of the people*. Cambridge, Massachusetts: Harvard University Press.
LENZ, H. 1964. *Vergliechende Psychiatrie. Ein Studie ueber die Beziehung von Kultur, Soziologie und Psychopathologie*. Wien: W. Maudrich.
LEVI-STRAUSS, C. 1949. Les structures élémentaires de la parenté. Paris: Presses Universitaires de France.
LEVI-STRAUSS, C. 1962a. *Le totémisme aujourd'hui*. Paris: Presses Universitaires de France.
LEVI-STRAUSS, C. 1962b. *La pensée sauvage*. Paris: Plon.
LEVI-STRAUSS, C. 1964. *Mythologiques I: Le cru et le cuit*. Paris: Plon.
LEVI-STRAUSS, C. 1966. *Mythologiques II: Du miel aux cendres*. Paris: Plon.
LEWIN, B. 1958. Die Konfliktneurose der Mohammerdanerin in Ägypten. *Zeitschrift fuer Psychotherapie und Medizin*. 8: 98-112.
LEWIS, O. 1959. *Five families: Mexican case studies in the culture of poverty*. New York: Basic Books.
LEWIS, O. 1961. *The children of Sanchez. Autobiography of a Mexican family*. New York: Random House.
LEWIS, O. 1964. *Pedro Martinez*. New York: Random House.
LOWIE, R. H. 1937. The history of ethnological theory. New York: Farrar and Rinehart.
MALINOWSKI, B. 1925. Mother-right and the sexual ignorance of savages. *International Journal of Psycho-Analysis*, 6: 109-130.
MALINOWSKI, B. 1926. *Crime and custom in savage society*. New York: Harcourt, Brace and Co.
MALINOWSKI, B. 1927. *Sex and repression in savage society*. New York: Humanities Press.
MCCLELLAND, D. C., and FRIEDMAN, G. A. 1952. A cross-cultural study of the relationship between child training practices and achievement motivation appearing in folk tales. In G. E. Swanson, T. N. Newcomb, and E. L. Hartley (Eds.), *Readings in social psychology*. New York: Henry Holt. Pp. 243-249.
MEAD, M. 1928. *Coming of age in Samoa*. New York: W. Morrow.
MEAD, M. 1930. *Growing up in New Guinea*. New York: W. Morrow.
MEAD, M. 1934. The use of primitive material in the study of personality. *Character and Personality*, 3: 10.
MEAD, M. 1935. *Sex and temperament in three primitive societies*. New York: W. Morrow.
MEAD, M. 1939. *From the South Seas*. New York: W. Morrow.
MEAD, M. 1940. The Mountain Arapesh. II: Supernaturalism. *Anthropological Papers of the American Museum of Natural History*. 37: 330-331.
MEAD, M. 1952. Some relationships between social anthropology and psychiatry. In F. Alexander and H. Ross (Eds.), *Dynamic Psychiatry*. Chicago: the University of Chicago Press. Pp. 401-448.

MEAD, M., and BATESON, G. 1942. *Balinese character.* New York Academy of Science. Special Publications 2.

MEAD, M., and McGREGOR, F. C. 1951. *Growth and culture. A photographic study of Balinese childhood.* New York: G. P. Putnam's Sons.

MEKEEL, H. S. 1943. Education, child training and culture. *Amer. J. Soc.,* 48: 676-681.

MERTON, R. K. 1938. Social structure and anomie. *Amer. Sociol. Rev.,* 3: 672-682.

METZGER, E. 1897. Einiges ueber Amok und Mataglap. *Globus,* 52: 107-110.

MINTZ, S. 1960. *Worker in the cane: A Puerto Rican life history.* New Haven, Connecticut: Yale University Press.

MURPHY, H. B. M. 1961. Social change and mental health. *The Milbank Memorial Fund Quarterly,* 39: 385-445.

MURPHY, H. B. M., WITTKOWER, E. D., and CHANCE, N. A. 1967. Cross-cultural inquiry into the symptomatology of depression: A preliminary report. *International Journal of Psychiatry,* 3: 6-22.

MURPHY, J. M. 1962. Cross-cultural studies of the prevalence of psychiatric disorders. *World Mental Health,* 14: 1-13.

OESTERREICHER, W. 1950. Manisch-depressive psychose bijeen Soendanese. *Med. Maandbl. Djakarta,* 3: 173-175.

OLIVER, S. C. 1965. Individuality, freedom of choice and cultural flexibility of the Kamba. *American Anthropologist,* 67: 421-428.

OPLER, M. K. 1936a. Some points of comparison and contrast between the treatment of functional disorders by Apache shamans and modern psychiatric practice. *American Journal of Psychiatry,* 92: 1371-1387.

OPLER, M. K. 1936b. An interpretation of ambivalence of two American Indian tribes. *Journal of Social Psychology,* 7: 82-116.

OPLER, M. K. 1938. Further comparative anthropological data bearing on the solution of a psychological problem. *Journal of Social Psychology,* 9: 447-483.

PARSONS, A. 1961. Some comparative observations on ward social structure: Southern Italy, England and the United States. *Transcultural Psychiatric Research Review,* No. 10: 65-67.

PARSONS, T. 1951a. *The social system.* Glencoe, Illinois: The Free Press.

PARSONS, T. 1951b. Illness and the role of the physician: A sociological perspective. *American Journal of Orthopsychiatry,* 21: 452-460.

PFEIFFER, W. M. 1969. Die Symptomatik der Depression in transkultureller Sicht. In H. Hippius and H. Selbach (Eds.), *Das depressive Syndrom.* Muenchen, Berlin, Wien: Urban and Schwarzenberg.

RADIN, P. 1913. Personal reminiscences of a Winnebago Indian. *Journal of American Folklore,* 26: 293-318.

RADIN, P. 1920. Crashing thunder, the autobiography of a Winnebago Indian. *University of California Publications in American Archaeology and Ethnology,* 16: 381-473.

RASCH, C. 1894. Ueber Amok. *Neurologisches Zentralblatt,* 13: 550-554.

RIN, H. 1963. Koro: A consideration on Chinese concepts of illness and case illustrations. *Transcultural Psychiatric Research Review,* No. 15: 23-30.

RIVERS, W. H. R. 1926. *Psychology and Ethnology.* London: Kegan Paul.

ROHEIM, G. 1850. *Psychoanalysis and anthropology.* New York: International Universities Press.

SAPIR, E. 1932. Cultural anthropology and psychiatry. *Journal of Abnormal Social Psychology,* 27: 229-242.

SAPIR, E. 1934. The emergence of the concept of personality in a study of culture. *Journal of Social Psychology,* 5: 408-415.

SAPIR, E. 1937. The contribution of psychiatry to an understanding of behavior in society. *American Journal of Sociology,* 42: 862-870.

SAPIR, E. 1938. Why cultural anthropology needs the psychiatrist. *Psychiatry.* 1: 7-12.

SAPIR, E. 1939. Psychiatric and cultural pitfalls in the business of getting a living. *Mental Health,* Publication No. 9. American Association for the Advancement of Science. Pp. 237-244.

SCHUBERT, A. 1930. Drawings of Orotchen children and young people. *Journal of Genetic Psychology,* 37: 232-244.

SCHWARTZ, T. 1962. The Paliau movement in the Admiralty Island, 1946-1954. *Anthropological Papers of the American Museum of Natural History,* 49: 207-422.

SELIGMAN, C. G. 1924. Anthropology and psychology. *Journal of the Royal Anthropological Institute of Great Britain and Ireland,* 54: 13-46.

SELIGMAN, C. G. 1929. Temperament, conflict and psychosis in a stone-age population. *British Journal of Medical Psychology,* 9: 187-202.

SPIEGEL, J. P. 1959. Some cultural aspects of transference and countertransference. In J. H. Masserman (Ed.), *Individual and family dynamics.* New York: Grune and Stratton, Pp. 160-182.

TURNER, V. W. 1969. *The ritual process: Structure and anti-structure* University Press.

TURNER, V. W. 1969. *The ritual profess: Structure and anti-structure.* Chicago: Aldine.

VAN BRERO, P. C. Z. 1895. Latah. *Journal of Mental Science.* p. 537.

VAN WULFFTEN-PALTHE, P. 1936. Psychiatry and neurology in the tropics. In A. Liechtenstein (Ed.), *A clinical textbook of tropical medicine.* Batavia: de Langen.

WALLACE, A. F. C. 1956. Revitalization movements: Some theoretical considerations for their comparative study. *American Anthropologist,* 58: 264-281.

WALLACE, A. F. C. 1959. The institutionalization of cathartic and control strategies in Iroquois religious psychotherapy. In M. K. Opler (Ed.), *Culture and mental health.* New York: Macmillan. Pp. 63-96.

WALLACE, A. F. C. 1961. *Culture and personality.* New York: Random House.

WEAKLAND, J. H. 1956. Orality in Chinese conceptions of male genital sexuality. *Psychiatry,* 19: 237-247.

WHITING, J. W. M. 1959. Sorcery, sin and the superego: A cross-cultural study of some mechanisms of social control. In M. R. Jones (Ed.), *Symposium on motivation.* Lincoln, Nebraska: University of Nebraska Press. Pp. 174-195.

WHITING, J. W. M. 1961. Socialization process and personality. In F. L. K. Hsu (Ed.), *Psychological anthropology*. Homewood, Illinois: The Dorsey Press. Pp. 355-380.

WHITING, J. W. M., and CHILD, I. L. 1953. *Child training and personality*. New Haven, Connecticut: Yale University Press.

WITTKOWER, E. D., MURPHY, H. B. M., FRIED, J. and ELLENBERGER, H. 1960. A cross-cultural inquiry into the symptomatology of schizophrenia. *Annals of the New York Academy of Sciences*, 84: 854-863.

WRIGHT, G. O. 1954. Projection and displacement: A cross-cultural study of folktale aggression. *Journal of Abnormal and Social Psychology*, 49: 523-528.

YAP, P. M. 1969. The culture-bound reactive syndrome. In W. Caudill and Tsung-yi Lin (Eds.), *Journal of Abnormal and Social Psychology*, Honolulu: East-West Center Press. Pp. 33-53.

2

Anthropology, Psychiatry, and Man's Nature

ROBERT B. EDGERTON, Ph.D.

Social Science Research Institute
University of Hawaii

From the early days when Malinowski and Ernest Jones quarreled over what each took to be the other's faulty comprehension of the Oedipus complex, anthropologists and psychiatrists viewed each other with no little disdain until sometime in the 1930's when, as Edward Sapir voiced it (1), anthropology began to recognize its need for psychiatric insight and collaboration. This interest brought together many pairs of anthropologists and psychiatrists or psychoanalysts—Sapir and Sullivan, Kluckhohn and Murray, Mekeel and Eriksen, Chapple and Lindemann to name but a few; and perhaps most significant, Linton and Kardiner. Out of these and other collaborations came the "Culture and Personality" episode, some of the excesses of which led much of anthropology to reject psychiatric theory and method as being well beyond the pale of acceptable scholarship or science (2). With the growth of transcultural psy-

I wish to acknowledge the assistance of the Social Science Research Institute (NIMH Grant MH 09243), University of Hawaii, during the preparation of this paper.

chiatry in the 1950's, psychiatrists turned to anthropology for consultation in difficult problems of cultural comparison. Anthropologists, as before, provided an imposing array of anecdotal instances to demonstrate the wondrous variety of man's culture and behavior—either in health or in sickness—and modern psychiatry became well versed in the language of cultural relativism and cultural determinism. Today, with the advent of social and community psychiatry and a host of innovations in treatment, anthropologists and psychiatrists find themselves engaged in joint research reflecting an astonishing variety of interests in epidemiology, etiology and treatment as well as such pressing current problems as poverty and urban blight, environmental deterioration, radical unrest, juvenile drug abuse, civil rights and issues of war and peace.

All of these mutual interests, today and over the past 50 years, have been and continue to be discussed in symposia and articles that appear with indefatigable regularity. So vast and diverse is the resulting literature that it cannot easily be characterized (3). Much of it is sectarian apologetics. Much of it is programmatic and empty. But some of it demonstrates that anthropology and psychiatry are capable of learning from one another and that today the two disciplines have a better understanding of each other's theories and working procedures than ever before. And yet it is obvious that misunderstanding remains and that the ever-expanding dominion of anthropology (for example, over modern urban societies, long the preserve of sociologists) and of psychiatrists (over virtually every aspect of human existence) threatens to lead both disciplines away from their most fundamental theoretical concerns.

It is to one of these common concerns, and I think a most fundamental one, that I wish to direct my remarks. I believe that both anthropology and psychiatry have as a basic concern what is often known as the Hobbesian question of order. The question can be phrased in various complementary ways. For example, "How is it that man is able to follow the rules of society?" or, "How is it that man sometimes fails to follow these rules?" (4) On the one hand, we ask about social order; on the other, we ask about social deviance and social disorganization (both of which may underlie or subsume mental illness).

Let me summarize the alternative answers that the social sciences currently give to Hobbes' question. Speaking in general terms, there are four answers commonly in use: 1) biology, 2) sub-culture, 3) conflict and, 4) human nature. Needless to say, any such classification necessarily simplifies the realities of explanation in social science somewhat, but in this case, the simplification does little violence to the theories that are at issue (5).

First, there are biological answers to our fundamental question concerning why man sometimes performs deviant, or "anti-social," acts. These kinds of answers were long in disrepute, taking the form of "bad seed" or "criminal mind" explanations. In recent years, however, we have witnessed the increasing legitimization of answers that point to faulty genetics as in cases of Turner syndrome or an extra Y chromosome (6), to the effect of poor nutrition especially protein deficiency in infancy (7), and to birth traumata especially in hypoxia (8). These kinds of explanations seem to grow in frequency and perhaps in legitimacy everyday, but at the very best they constitute nothing more than a means of equating deviant behavior with the anomalous biology. Explanations that depend upon biological anomalies can never be expected to account for more than a small percentage of the cases of mental illness, theft, sexual misconduct, disbelief, or violence that can be described in any social system.

Subcultural answers to the Hobbesian question take this form: "People who violate the norms of a society do so because by conforming to their own way of life, they come into conflict with the culture of the dominant society."

Also known as the theory of differential association, this perspective says that men do not in fact commit deviant acts. They act in accord with their own cultural commitments, but, given the cultural pluralism of our modern nations, one man's cultural values may easily come into conflict with another's, and hence the dominant political group may come to define the moral behavior of subordinate groups as "deviant." This sort of explanation has served primarily as a means of accounting for the differences in delinquency and crime rates in ethnically diverse large cities.

The two remaining explanations carry with them quite different assumptions about human nature. Conflict theory assumes that man is a highly moral animal who not only respects the rules of his society, but internalizes them so that deviance from these rules is very difficult, even unthinkable under normal conditions. Given this assumption that man wants to conform, the cause of deviance must lie in a major dislocation of the social fabric, a dislocation in which man is "frustrated" or "alienated," "deprived" or "discontented." This view, most often associated with the sociologist Robert Merton, assumes that man will deviate from the expectations of his fellow men only if he experiences some major conflict between his goals and his means of attaining them.

The final theory assumes that man is naturally a deviant. This view follows more or less directly from Hobbes who saw men as deviants who were constrained primarily by fear. It sees social order not as a given, but as an accomplishment necessary to the control of men who would otherwise be engaged in the "war of all against all." In this theory, deviance is taken for granted, and order must be accounted for.

If we review these four major explanatory positions we will find quite discrepant views of human nature. Setting aside all explanations that combine these views into some sort of generic social learning theory position, we find these possibilities: 1) Biological deviance in which most men are natural conformists, but a few deviate because of their aberrant biology; 2) sub-cultural deviance in which all men are conformists, and deviance exists only due to cultural diversity and inequities in political power; 3) conflict deviance in which men are natural conformists who come to deviate only under conditions of social strain; and 4) human nature deviance in which men are naturally given to deviance and only strong means of social and cultural control can succeed in maintaining order.

These four alternatives are simplistic, but each exists, and is often expressed in just this form. To be sure, there are theories that combine these explanations, but these "multiple factor" positions usually do little to provide clearer or more sophisticated assumptions. Assuming then that these are the current views, which one predominates? There can be no doubt that the *least* favored view in social science today is that of deviance as a product of human nature—the view originally associated with Hobbes and later with Freud. In the dominant view, man is a natural conformist, and this position owes much to anthropology.

I

The anthropological discovery that men everywhere lived in well-ordered societies and yet had extraordinarily different beliefs and behaviors has been most significant, arguing as it does against any view of man as an animal by nature individualistic and difficult to socialize. What is more, despite such evident differences between societies, anthropologists reported that in any given society, behavior and even personality were quite homogeneous; and this fallacious view of the homogeneity of primitive society has persisted through the years despite many recent and past anthropological disclaimers. Again, it was argued, if all men in a society behave similarly, and if their society is well-ordered, then it must not be difficult to teach men to live within the rules of their society. Underlying this assumption was a still more basic one—that of *tabula rasa*. Locke's term, stated even more forcefully by Montesquieu and later given wide support by Dewey, probably received its greatest support from anthropologists, and from none more importantly than Margaret Mead. The *tabula rasa* assumption is regularly disavowed whenever it becomes explicit, but throughout social science, the assumption remains implicit: human infants are born sufficiently plastic that they can easily learn to live in any society.

Finally, and perhaps most importantly, anthropology provided a set of understandings associated with the folk-urban continuum. From Tönnies with his gemeinschaft-gesellschaft distinction, to von Gierke and Durkheim, through Maine, Weber, MacIver, Cooley and Becker, social science has developed a contrastive typology of folk versus urban dwellers. Such a typology was given its greatest currency in anthropology by Robert Redfield in his well-known folk-urban continuum (9). The details of this folk-urban contrast are not important here, but the general understanding is, for in anthropology and in social science generally we have come to accept the delusion of a folk-type society which is stable, homogeneous, and free of deviance or disruption. In contrast, the heterogeneity, deviance, and disorder of urban society are believed to be a direct consequence of the relative distance between these societies and the tranquil folk from which they have, perhaps unwisely, diverged.

The sociologist, Dennis Wrong, has called this conventional wisdom the "oversocialized view of man" (10). In this conventional view it is assumed that man wants to behave correctly for two reasons: because he internalizes his culture, and because he cherishes the esteem of his fellow men. These two sovereign mechanisms purport to explain—to the complete satisfaction of many—why order comes to pass. Therefore, it has become quite literally absurd to ask why social order exists (11). It is generally believed that the answer is obvious.

How have the social sciences reached this view of man in the face of Freud's insistence upon the need of the superego to constrain the id? How especially since Freud also noted that a great many men fail to acquire superegos, and hence are constrained, as Hobbes had it, solely by fear of external punishment? (12) I can only say that it is clear enough that the force of Freud's early emphasis upon biological motivation, and the id, was gradually eroded away by neo-Freudian amendments, and that modern psychiatric theory, reflecting prevailing general social science theory, has given less and less credence to the Freudian view that man is a natural deviant (13). Instead, as in conflict theory, the sources of deviance, as of psychopathology in general, are found to lie in the social and cultural environment. This environmentalist perspective has come to dominate even in psychoanalysis. For example, Judd Marmor, writing in *Modern Psychoanalysis*, says: "In advanced psychoanalytic circles today the focus of psychopathology is no longer being sought—at least to the same degree as formerly—within the individual's psyche, but rather in his system of relationships, his family, his small groups, his community, his society" (14).

At the same time that the causal force of the social and cultural environment has been accorded complete dominion over man, evaluations that separate good and bad environments have become commonplace. It is a simple matter to discover, as in the work of Erich Fromm (15), that some psychiatrists hold almost Rousseauian views about the beneficent environment of folk societies, while they regard urban environments with undisguised alarm, pointing to social disorganization and mental illness as the more or less inevitable consequences of faulty urban environment. Although many others say little about the infrequency of mental illness in folk societies (psychiatrists seem decidedly unsure of this matter today), they make it very clear that cities are pathogenic environments in which mental illness flourishes, and they seem to think that they know how to alter cities so that the incidence of mental illness will decrease (16).

I confess that I am not certain what psychiatrists read in anthropology these days (the residents whom I teach read next to nothing), but my impression is that while psychiatrists used to read a fair amount of anthropology—at least the more accessible sort—they now tend to get their anthropology secondhand through the writings of other psychiatrists. Nevertheless, I would still suspect that their ideas, and all ideas in behavioral science, are colored by the pervasive assumptions of the folk-urban contrast. It is the adequacy of this comparison that I wish to examine here.

Briefly stated, the folk-urban comparison insists that whereas cities are culturally diverse and socially disorganized, folk societies are homogeneous in thought and action and their social order is well integrated; further, cities are said to be impersonal with great tolerance for individuality, whereas folk societies are personal with little individual variability; also, it is assumed that while the folk know what their culture is—what is expected of them—and are well able to behave as they should, that city dwellers are often unsure what is expected of them, and therefore lack the ability (or the desire) to behave as they should; finally, the stresses of life in cities produce many maladapted or mentally ill people, while life in folk societies produces many fewer mental illnesses. The ideal of the folk society was stated to perfection by Jane Belo, as she wrote some years ago about the island of Bali: "The babies do not cry, the small boys do not fight, the young girls bear themselves with decorum, the old men dictate with dignity. Everyone carries out his appointed task, with respect for his equals and superiors, and gentleness and consideration for his dependents. The people adhere, apparently with ease, to the laws governing the actions, big and small, of their lives (1935: 141)." Unfortunately, for those who would like to take this idyllic vision to heart, Belo went on, I presume unwittingly, to document contrary instances in which men beat their wives, wives berate husbands and leave home, children quarrel with their parents, and men and women alike rebel against the constraints of Balinese custom and authority (17).

Although anthropologists have long recognized that primitive man does express individuality, many continue to write as if this knowledge were of little theoretical importance. And in behavioral science outside of anthropology, there is ample evidence that many believe primitive man to be truly the slave of society, or as someone once put it, the men in the grey flannel loin-cloths. We in anthropology are largely responsible for this state of affairs, and, however unintentionally, we have perpetuated it by many of our practices. When we write about primitive life, we often generalize to such a degree that all individual variability is lost in our search for patterns and our enthusiastic construction of models. Since we are in the business of searching for regularities of culture, we not only often fail to record variability, we sometimes even fail to see it when it is right before our eyes. What is worse, when we have attempted to make theoretical sense out of our cultural materials we have often distorted them by omitting reference to discrepant beliefs, deviant behaviors and organizational anomalies because we have been committed to a generic theory of equilibrium which has literally compelled us to find a positive social function for everything that we see. All this we have done, but sociology has also contributed to the myth of folk-urban contrast in many ways. By way of brief example, I should mention the tremendously influential writings of Talcott Parsons on the level of grand theory, and at the empirical level, the work of the dominant Chicago school of social deviance. The effects of both kinds of writings have been to reduce awareness of cultural ambiguity and behavioral variability (18).

I cannot leave this subject without making reference to the impact of Margaret Mead. Read by millions in and out of the social and psychological sciences, she has probably done more than any other person to enhance understanding of cultural diversity *and* of human plasticity. In her efforts to show, for example, that male and female roles are a product of culture, not biology, and that thought processes and adolescence too are cultural, she has impressed an immense audience with the dominance of culture over biology. But she has also written persuasively of the individuality that somehow manages to persist despite the force of folk culture. For example, she wrote this of the folk society of Manu'a, in Samoa: "The Manu'an culture presents such a striking picture of flexibility, rapid slight changes, easy acceptance of innovation and deviation, that it would seem to give each gifted individual a particularly open field for the exercise of his peculiar talents." But she also wrote of the force of culture over the individual, saying this of her efforts to convey this message: "The battle which we once had to fight with the whole battery at our command, with the most fantastic and startling examples we could muster, is now won. As the devout in the Middle Ages would murmur a precautionary 'God Willing' before stating a plan or a wish, those who write about the problems of man and society have learned to insert a precautionary 'in our culture' . . ." (20). This may well have been a Pyrrhic victory, for while Mead's emphasis on culture has done much to make the dominance of culture over man common knowledge, her observations regarding human individuality and deviance have gone largely unnoticed.

II

What are the facts of man's behavior in folk societies? Are men in the world's smallest, simplest and most isolated societies slaves to their culture? Do they readily accept constraint? Or do they seek to express their individuality? We now possess enough information about such societies that we can begin to answer such questions with reasonable confidence. Although I am preparing a fully developed treatment of these questions in a book that is now underway, for present purposes, I can do no more than sketch the outlines of behavior in such societies.

Small, technologically simple, nonliterate, culturally isolated societies once constituted man's only way of life. Even today, such societies survive in many parts of the world, and our records of these societies and others like them that were studied earlier in this century provide us with accounts of life in some several dozen societies in which men live solely by hunting and gathering, and in several dozen more in which life depends upon shifting horticulture. When we include larger tribal societies, and peasant farmers who live on the fringes of modern nation states, we have reasonably adequate records for several hundreds of cultures.

It is true that in all of these societies there is an easily discerned social and cultural order. Men live by cultural rules. Some of these rules can be stated explicitly, others are followed unswervingly even though they are never stated and may be unconscious. There are rules against murder, and these are generally followed. And there are obvious patterns of speech, of gesture, of posture and of perception which are also deeply ingrained. All this we have seen and recorded. In emphasizing the wondrous diversity of human cultures, and the dominion of culture over man's behavior, however, we have tended to overlook the equally obvious fact that in all of these societies, man is never simply a creature of his culture. On the contrary, in all societies, some aspects of culture are ambiguous, behavior varies greatly from person to person, some of this behavioral variation violates the existing rules—and about all this men argue, negotiate and arbitrate. I would like to expand upon each of these points.

1) *Ambiguity.* First, it must be obvious that no society has ever stated all of its important rules, much less all of its culture, in any explicit code. Furthermore, no society has ever held all of its members strictly accountable for all of their actions, so that each breach of a norm carried with it inevitable and identical punishment. Instead, we find that in folk societies, as in our own, rules are often very fuzzy around the edges, being relative to the situation, the actor and the audience, and leaving ample room for disagreement and negotiation about what is or is not just and proper (21).

For example, we hear this about village life in Thailand: "The first characteristic of Thai culture to strike an observer from the West, or from Japan or Vietnam, is the individualistic behavior of the people. The longer one resides in Thailand the more one is struck by the almost determined lack of regularity, discipline and regimentation in Thai life" (22). Or we hear this about the nature of culture among the Kamba of Kenya: "There seems to be what is almost a conscious avoidance of *specificity* in many of the principles of Kamba culture. The rules are often vague and open-ended. They tend to be quite general, and a person is expected to make his own interpretation of them. The 'right thing' to do *should* emerge from argument and discussion, and the argument, though loosely structured, is by no means predetermined" (23).

Examples such as these that reflect the ambiguity and indeterminacy of cultural rules are found throughout the literature on the folk societies of the world. The Pygmies of the Ituri forest in the Congo often argue over their culture, with agreement sometimes far too much to hope for (24); The Paliyans of South India, a small and isolated society, display a truly impressive lack of agreement concerning many of their cultural norms, apparently achieving relative consensus only where rules concerning violence are at issue (25). Similar examples abound, as, for example, from Choiseul in Melanesia (26), in Ceylon (27), Village India (28), the Siriono of South America (29), or the Eskimo (30).

To emphasize this ambiguity, I might mention the research of Tyler who has shown that even our long inviolate kinship terms, those solid and clear rules upon which so many anthropological analyses have rested, are anything but simple and clear-cut. Instead they vary greatly with the situation and with the intention of the speaker, to mention only two of the variables that complicate what had been thought to be a standard set of words and understandings (31).

Finally, I mention the Walbiri, Australian aborigines of the central desert. The culture of these people is often said to be among the most simple, or folk-like, known. Yet, it has long been recognized that Walbiri religious and kinship systems are exceedingly complex. What is more, these systems are ambiguous, with the rules regarding whom a man should or could marry being anything but unequivocal. Meggitt comments as follows:

> "Facts of this sort indicate that, although we may draw neat diagrams to illustrate the ideal relations existing among persons, patrilines, lodges, subsections and patrimoieties, the real-life situations are not necessarily as rigidly structured as the diagrams suggest. The deviations from the norms that occasionally occur do not greatly perturb the people, and eventually the anomalous case is fitted into the framework. Such discrepancies, moreover, are not a recent product of social disorganization following European contact; the very complexity of Walbiri social structure made it inevitable that there would always be some individuals who could not, or would not, follow all the rules" (32).

2) *Behavioral Variability.* But it is not simply that there are certain individuals who cannot or will not follow the rules. The great flexibility of some rules permits a wide range of "normal," that is, acceptable, variability. In fact, the expression of individual variability in conduct can become so pronounced in some very small societies that the discovery of rules becomes very difficult indeed. It is this point that Levi-Strauss makes when he says of the Nambikwara, a small South American society, "The society of the Nambikwara had been reduced to the point at which I found nothing but human beings" (33).

This range of behavior seen among individuals in folk societies has made efforts to describe a typical or modal personality far more difficult than any of our dominant theories of socialization would lead us to expect (34). As Kaplan and Lindzey, two leading students of projective test results among non-Western peoples have concluded independently (35), the range of personality variables among folk populations is every bit as great as it is in the large and "heterogeneous" societies of the West. Observational accounts of personality differentiation confirm this impression of great diversity among folk populations (36).

Students of primate behavior have reported the same sort of diversity: "Most field workers in primatology have been impressed with individual variations in characteristic patterns of interaction among the members of social groups of nonhuman primates, and have reported their observations under the various captions of personality, temperament, character, and comportment" (37).

While there is little argument over the anthropological contention that culture is man's means of adapting to his environment, we would do well to doubt that culture must be rigid and constraining and must greatly restrict human individuality if man is successfully to adapt. The evidence from the smallest folk societies strongly suggests that individual variation flourishes to the same degree that it does among primates. From a Ceylonese community (38), to a tribe in Western Uganda (39), to the Crow of the American plains (40), to much of New Guinea (41), evidence of individual diversity in many areas of behavior is plentiful. Indeed, in reviewing 26 hunting and gathering societies around the world, Gardner concluded that, "The very extreme individualism found among food gathering tribes contrasts with the lesser individualism of so-called individualist complex societies" (42).

3) *Deviance.* It is also the case that this individuality often goes beyond acceptable limits and becomes generally condemned or punished. In such cases we may appropriately speak of deviance. The literature has long contained accounts of deviant individuals in many of the world's folk societies, but I do not believe it is generally recognized even today that deviance occurs so frequently or in so many domains of human life. It is now clear, I believe, that not a few individuals, but many, maintain highly iconoclastic beliefs about what their society most highly values or holds sacred, and there are many others who act upon their deviant beliefs by violating the fundamental rules of their society. To take but a few examples of many, we have Turnbull's account of a Pygmy band in the isolated Ituri forest—as small and remote a folk society as the world can now offer. Among the many highly deviant acts that Turnbull reports, I mention that of a man who flagrantly violated the rules regarding cooperation in hunting by secretly setting up his net in front of those of the other Pygmies; he was found out and punished, but was subsequently restored to his previous position in the society, and, later committed other deviant acts (43). Or, we might mention deviance among the Bushmen, another small, isolated folk society, this time in South Africa's Kalahari desert. For the Bushmen, sharing food is a prime value, one that is given strong sanction. Yet Thomas reports that children sometimes refuse to share their food,

and that some adults sometimes take advantage of their more industrious and generous kinsmen (44).

In similar folk societies, more flagrant acts such as murder, rape and arson also occur—and sometimes go unpunished (45). In some folk societies, such offenses as theft are virtually epidemic, despite sanctions against thievery. In others, theft is quite rare, but nonetheless sometimes occurs. Langness reports a man among the Bena-Bena of Highland New Guinea who was a habitual and flagrant thief, but was otherwise a respected and competent member of the society. His thievery was objected to, and sometimes was punished, but it continued and the only explanation given by other Bena for his conduct was that he was a man who was, by nature, a thief (46). And, needless to say, there are those whose violations of the legitimate norms take place for no good reason, and therefore become recognized as evidence of severe mental illness (47).

I cannot possibly provide an adequate review of the magnitude or variety of deviance in folk societies here, and at present the literature contains no such review (48). Consequently, I can only assert that older conceptions (such as those held by Benedict and others) which saw folk societies as places in which the overwhelming majority of persons led deviance-free lives and only a handful became deviants is clearly incorrect. Instead, it is clear that a substantial number of persons in these societies commit deviant acts at one time or another during their lives and that a fair number of individuals become labelled as deviant persons. It is equally significant that the consequences of such deviance are highly unpredictable.

4) *The Negotiability of Deviant Acts.* It is undeniably the case that many who deviate from their societies' norms meet with stern, sometimes even lethal, opposition. Witches, murderers, arsonists, psychotics—all commonly encounter fatal contretemps. But it is not always so. There are a great many recorded instances of individuals who have deviated

most flagrantly, yet have lived to enjoy the profits of their deviance. A well-quoted example is provided by Pospisil, who recounts the case of a New Guinea headman whose desire to add yet another local beauty to his collection of comely wives led him to violate his society's incest rules, with the result that he was forced to flee his community to escape the murderous wrath of various outraged citizens. Nevertheless, after a series of discussions among interested parties, he was able to return, none the worse for wear, and indeed, he resumed his position of power fully able to exploit his advantage. The result was a radical alteration in his society's rules regarding incest (49).

A comparable case is available from Africa in Lindblom's account of the Kamba, Kisese, who imbibed altogether too much, then attempted to return home only to pass out in a convenient hut. Unfortunately for Kisese, he chose to collapse in the worst possible place—the house of his mother-in-law. Among these tribesmen, as among many folk people, a man must avoid his mother-in-law or suffer humiliation and excessive fine. For the Kamba so extreme was this avoidance that a man might hurl himself into a thornbush rather than risk a meeting with his mother-in-law along a path. In Kisese's case, matters were desperate. When he awoke, it was already morning and a goodly crowd had gathered to witness his discomfort, and to discuss his subsequent legal embarrassment. Kisese was a man of wealth and power, however, and when he realized his predicament, he simply removed himself from the forbidden house and announced airily that he had no intention of paying any fine whatever, and that as far as he was concerned the custom was foolish and should be abolished. Amazingly—and almost certainly only because other men of substance also found the rule onerous—Kisese went unpunished, and the rule was henceforth greatly attenuated in its force (50).

The negotiability of deviant acts is nicely illustrated by so-called wild-man behavior in Highland New Guinea, where

men appear to misbehave in order to achieve a reduction in
their economic responsibilities (51), or in East Africa, where
men sometimes plead mental illness to excuse their flagrant
violations of the moral and legal order (52), or by the general practice of reserving verbal or physical aggression for
occasions when drunkenness may serve to mitigate the of-
fence (53). The complex matters of arbitration and negotiation are seen in rich, naturally occurring detail in Goldschmidt's account of the legacy of an African herdsman
(54).

Sometimes, of course, the sanctions against deviant behavior are supernatural, consisting of immediate and horrible
punishment by gods, spirits, ancestors or the like. Thus it
was in many parts of Polynesia and Melanesia and so it was
among the Samburu in Kenya's Northern Frontier area.
Among the Samburu, a warlike, cattle herding people,
little deviance is permissible, and serious deviance is subject
to supernatural sanction in the form of a curse, the efficacy
of which literally no one doubts. Yet Spencer reports a case
in which a man breached the rules, confronted the curse,
achieved his end, and after twenty years, had gotten away
with his audacious behavior (55).

Even in societies like the Samburu, where individuality
or deviance is restricted, we find extraordinary evidence that
men will nonetheless manage to intrude a certain amount of
discretion into their notions of punishment. For example,
the Walbiri of Australia are as small, as isolated and as apparently inflexible a society as any of which we have record.
Meggitt writes that their jural norms permit little flexibility
or uncertainty, adding that justice is done with remarkably
little opportunity for the exercise of privilege or power (56).
Nevertheless, and virtually in spite of himself, he writes that
these Australian aborigines adjudicate their cases of deviant
behavior by taking into account "community membership,
kinship and friendship" and that these considerations "are
likely to bias the individual's judgment." (57) He adds, by

now anticlimactically, that "a person's reputation, and not his present behavior alone, may determine the treatment accorded him. . . ." (58) And so it often is, everywhere.

The point of these examples is this: neither external sanctions nor internal constraints always succeed in preventing the expression of misconduct. Among simpler societies, in fact, the internal sanction, guilt, seems rarely to operate to constrain behavior, although shame is typically a very effective source of control. What is more, supernatural sanctions are by no means always swift and terrible; they must often be reinforced by various human interventions. And, most apparent of all, all human systems of social control, from formal legal systems to primitive councils and moots and "public opinion," are susceptible to influence by the powerful, and suasion by persons who can claim such advantages as kinship, friendship or economic patronage.

In summary, it can be said that all this—ambiguity, variability, deviance and negotiated consequences—is characteristic of hunting and gathering and tribal horticultural and pastoral societies. This is not to say, of course, that all these societies are alike in their tolerance for ambiguity and individuality. There appear to be differences of degree and kind among these societies that can be related to such differing environmental conditions as relative involvement in warfare or economic cooperation. I might add here that while my analysis is far from complete, it is my impression that among peasant societies—those technologically simple, agricultural societies within large state systems—the expression of individuality is typically somewhat less pronounced than it is among tribal societies. At the very least, it appears that great differences may exist, as for example between the Chinese village studied by Yang where little deviance is reported (59), and the Chinese village as seen by Wolf where deviance occurs in many overt and covert forms (60). Or, for another example, we might compare the Greeks of Sarakatsani among whom deviance is abhorred and seldom expressed

(61), or those of Vasilika who have developed an extraordinarily flexible and individuated way of life (62).

But perhaps some of the apparent difference can be attributed to differences in the perspectives of those who study these peoples, as we have seen in the contrasting reports of the Mexican folk society of Tepoztlán. Redfield's study of Tepoztlán emphasized its tranquil, contented people living a life of almost ideal social integration and individual adjustment (61); Lewis, who studied the same society some years later, reported social conflict complete with individual fear, hatred, distrust, violence, and suffering (63). It might appear that the two reports could scarcely be more discrepant, and yet both *could* be correct—as Redfield himself has admitted (63). The point is not simply that human observers are projective systems, or that all human observation suffers from a reactive Heisenberg effect. The point is that individuality and deviance can, and usually do, exist within a social or cultural order that appears—from another perspective, to be well-integrated and smoothly functioning. It is only when we equate deviance with disorganization that we doom ourselves to perpetual misunderstanding.

III

So ubiquitous is human individuality and deviance, so irrepressible is man's willfulness, that no one who is serious about a theory of human behavior can fail to take these considerations into account. Individuality and deviance may result from social conflict, from cultural diversity or from biological disorder, but none of these alone, or in combination, is sufficient as an explanation of the deviance that exists in the world's societies. That is so because deviance occurs, and often, in societies where there is no discernible social conflict or strain and no cultural diversity, and such deviance is far too common to be a product of faulty biology. On the contrary, it must reflect *normal* biology; deviance must be part of man's nature. While I grant that there has as yet been no demonstration of this thesis, I am confident that the thesis is correct, and that a demonstration is possible.

We can no longer afford the luxury enjoyed in the earlier days of social science when we chose to assume that whatever man's nature might be it was so thoroughly malleable that only nurture need be focused upon the overwhelmingly dominant partner in the nature/nurture opposition. I believe that it is no longer reasonable to ignore the fact that man has a nature which is not entirely tractable and which continues to assert itself no matter *what* form his culture may take. One aspect of his nature is willfulness, and a concern with self-interest that leads, when conditions are right, to deviance.

However, even if you grant me the truth of this assertion, it does not necessarily follow that Hobbes was right— that man is so implacable an opponent of society that only the Leviathan can tame him. Such a one-sided view of man cannot possible represent all that we see in human behavior. Instead, we would do better to turn to Aristotle, who referred to man as both angel and beast, for it is undeniably the case that man is both of these things. It is this duality, and complexity, of his nature that we must seek to understand.

And this leads to my central point. It is empirically the case that man everywhere lives in societies which maintain themselves by giving sanction to certain rules, yet they build ambiguity into many of those rules and permit some deviance from them. As long as we regard order and deviance as incompatible—as polar extremes on a folk-urban continuum—we will fail to understand what is the essential truth: that man is by nature both a deviant and a conformist. I have attempted to argue in this paper that man is often given to the expression of individuality, and of willful self-interest even when this interest runs counter to the values of his society. There should be no need to document the complementary fact that man requires security—as an infant and an adult—that he seeks cognitive consonance and affective assurance, and that he must often subordinate his will to others, and that he is capable of love and self-sacrifice. All this, of course, is well-known and has been elegantly stated by many, not the least of whom was Freud.

This understanding leads to a basic distinction. If one assumes that man is not tractable, not malleable, not easily made to live with his fellow men, then certain other assumptions follow. One of the most important is this: social order is *not* a given, it is an accomplishment, and by no means an easy one. To accomplish social order, man's dual nature must be appeased; thus, while the system must provide predictability and security it must do so while providing an optimum of flexibility. The sociologist, Etzioni, has referred to this requirement as "the need for variance in a social structure," and has referred to it as a "second-order need" of man (64). A. K. Cohen has put it this way: "Every system can tolerate a certain amount of ambiguity, uncertainty, and even confusion, and there are no doubt many rules that regulate conduct with such precision and detail that they thwart rather than facilitate the accomplishment of human purposes." (65) I would add this: Durkheim was right when he said that every cultural rule creates its own potential for deviance; but this is merely an exercise in logic. It is more important to say that man creates rules that provide him with security and predictability, at the same time that he creates other rules that permit him to express choice and to achieve personal advantage; and then man sometimes violates these rules, not merely because the violation of any rule is inherent in that rule's definition, but because a refusal to live at all times within society's rules is inherent in man.

Unfortunately, we are all reduced to asserting such basic truths rather than demonstrating them, for many of the essential supporting data are not yet in hand. That they are not is a result of many difficulties in theory and method, but it is also a result of the fact that both anthropology and psychiatry have ignored man's nature in favor of more topical and more epiphenomenal matters. However, in the social sciences, there is evidence that man's nature is no longer quite so tabooed a topic and that universals of behavior and biology are now beginning to receive serious study. (66)

If such a redirection of emphasis is to succeed, then certain research must be carried out and this research falls directly within the traditional province of psychiatry. Psychiatry has already contributed greatly to this concern, but much remains to be done. First, there must be far more done to study the relationship between biology and behavior. Much has already been accomplished in, for example, biochemistry and neurophysiology, and psychiatrists have made many of these contributions, but to derive the greatest benefit from such research, it must be designed in such a manner that the complex influence of the social and cultural environment can be effectively taken into account. Secondly, there is a compelling need for longitudinal studies of the process of socialization, studies in which both biology and environment are examined with equal seriousness. We have the beginnings of such research in the work of Thomas, Chess and colleagues (67), but these are only beginnings. Finally, we need clinically sensitive research into man's dual nature, as man himself can reveal it. We already have many such highly instructive accounts from the rich clinical literature already available in psychiatry. But we must also know how so-called normal men struggle with their natures; thus far, novelists have preempted a deserted field. The time for psychiatry to study all men—not merely "patients"—is long overdue.

Although David Humes was one of the first men properly to emphasize the undeniable fact that man is largely a product of his environment, he also saw that all sciences have a relationship to human nature, saying that "however wide any of them may seem to run from it, they still return back by one passage or another." (68) Anthropology has certainly fulfilled the first part of Hume's prophecy, our sciences will continue to stand upon a cornerstone of partial knowledge and assumption—hardly the most reliable building blocks for our already top-heavy edifice of knowledge.

REFERENCES

1. EDWARD SAPIR, "Why Cultural Anthropology Needs the Psychiatrist," *Psychiatry* 1: 7-12, 1938; "Cultural Anthropology and Psychiatry," *Journal of Abnormal and Social Psychology*, 27: 229-42, 1932.
2. For a convenient and excellent review, see: Milton Singer, "A Survey of Culture and Personality Theory and Research," In Bert Kaplan (ed.), *Studying Personality Cross-Culturally*, pp. 9-90. New York: Harper and Row, 1961.
3. For example, see: Ernest Jones, "Psychoanalysis and Anthropology," *Journal of the Royal Anthropological Institute*, 54: 47-66. 1924; Jules Henry, "Common Problems of Research in Anthropology and Psychiatry," *American Journal of Orthopsychiatry*, 18: 698-703, 1948; Clyde Kluckhohn, "The Influence of Psychiatry on Anthropology in America during the Past One Hundred Years," In J. K. Hall (ed.), *One Hundred Years of American Psychiatry*, pp. 569-617. New York: Columbia University Press, 1944; F. L. K. Hsu, "Anthropology or Psychiatry: A Definition of Objectives and their Implications," *Southwestern Journal of Anthropology*, 8: 227-250, 1952; George Devereaux, "Psychiatry and Anthropology," *Bulletin Menninger Clinic*, 16: 167-177, 1952; Silvano Arieti, "Some Basic Problems Common to Anthropology and Psychiatry," *American Anthropologist*, 58: 26-39, 1956; Ernest Becker, "The Relevance of Psychiatry to Recent Research in Anthropology," *American J. Psychotherapy*, 16: 600-617, 1962; and, Margaret Mead, "Problems and Progress in the Study of Personality," In Edward Norbeck, *et al* (eds.), *The Study of Personality: An Interdisciplinary Appraisal*, pp. 373-381. New York: Holt, Rinehart and Winston, 1968.
4. THOMAS HOBBES, *Leviathan.* New York: E. P. Dutton, 1950.
5. For discussion of social deviance, I recommend: A. K. Cohen, *Deviance and Control*, Englewood Cliffs, New Jersey: Prentice-Hall, Inc., 1966; Travis Hirschi, *Causes of Delinquency*. Berkeley, University of California Press, 1969; David Matza, *Becoming Deviant*, Englewood Cliffs, New Jersey: Prentice-Hall, 1969.
6. For example, see: Jerry Hirsch, (ed.), *Behavior Genetic Analysis.* New York: McGraw-Hill, 1967.

7. For example, see: J. M. Joffe, *Prenatal Determinants of Behavior.* Oxford Pergamon Press, 1969.

8. WILLIAM F. WINDLE, "Brain Damage by Asphyxia at Birth," *Scientific American,* 216: 77-84, 1969.

9. For example, see: Robert Redfield, "The Folk Society," *American J. of Sociology,* 52: 293-308, 1947; George Foster, "What is Folk Culture?" *American Anthropologist,* 55: 159-173, 1953; Robert Redfield, *The Little Community. Viewpoints for the Study of a Human Whole.* Chicago, University of Chicago Press, 1955.

10. DENNIS WRONG, "The Oversocialized Conception of Man in Modern Sociology," *American Sociological Review,* 26: 183-193, 1961.

11. *ibid.*

12. SIGMUND FREUD, *Civilization and its Discontents.* Trans. by Joan Riviere. London: L. and Virginia Woolf at the Hogarth Press, 1930.

13. *ibid.*

14. JUDD MARMOR, *Modern Psychoanalysis. New Directions and Perspectives.* New York: Basic Books, 1968. P. 4.

15. For example, see: Erich Fromm, *The Heart of Man.* New York: Harper and Row, 1964.

16. For example, see: Edward Stainbrook, "Society and Individual Behavior," In Benjamin Wolman (ed.), pp. 216-231, *Handbook of Clinical Psychology.* New York: McGraw-Hill, 1965; L. J. Duhl, (ed.), *The Urban Condition.* New York: Basic Books, 1963.

17. JANE BELO, "The Balinese Temper," *Character and Personality,* 4: 120-146, 1935, p. 144.

18. For a similar assertion, see D. Matza, 1969, op. cit.

19. MARGARET MEAD, "The Role of the Individual in Samoan Culture," *J. Royal Anthropological Institute of Great Britain and Ireland,* 58: 481-495, 1928, p. 481.

20. MARGARET MEAD, *From the South Seas.* New York: Wm. Morrow, 1939, p. x-xi.

21: See: H. L. A. Hart, *Punishment and Responsibility.* London: Oxford University Press, 1968; Craig MacAndrew and Robert B. Edgerton, *Drunken Comportment; A Social Explanation.* Chicago: Aldine, 1969.

22. JOHN EMBREE, "Thailand—A Loosely Structured Social System," *American Anthropologist,* 52: 181-193, 1950, p. 182.

23. SYMMES OLIVER, "Individuality, Freedom of Choice, and Cultural Flexibility of the Kamba," *American Anthropologist,* 67: 421-424, 1965, p. 427.

24. COLIN TURNBULL, *The Forest People.* New York: Simon and Schuster, 1961.

25. PETER GARDNER, "Symmetric Respect and Memorate Knowledge: The Structure and Ecology of Individualistic Culture," *Southwestern J. Anthropology,* 22: 389-415, 1966, p. 398.

26. HAROLD SCHEFFLER, *Choiseul Island Social Structure.* Berkeley: University of California Press, 1965.

27. EDMUND LEACH, *Pul Eliya. A Village in Ceylon.* London: Cambridge University Press, 1961.
28. ALAN BEALS, *Culture in Process.* New York: Holt, Rinehart and Winston, 1967.
29. A. R. HOLMBERG, *Nomads of the Long Bow.* Smithsonian Institution, Institute of Social Anthropology, publication 10, 1950.
30. KAI BIRKET-SMITH, *The Caribou Eskimos: Material and Social Life and Their Cultural Position.* Copenhagen: Gyldeddanske Boghandel, 1929.
31. STEPHEN TYLER, "Context and Variation in Koga Kinship Terminology," *American Anthropologist,* 68: 693-707, 1966.
32. M. J. MEGGITT, Desert People. *A Study of the Walbiri Aborigines of Central Australia.* Sydney: Angus and Robertson, 1963, p. 219.
33. CLAUDE LEVI-STRAUSS, *A World on the Wane.* Trans. by J. Russell. New York, Criterion, 1961.
34. A. F. C. WALLACE, *Culture and Personality.* New York: Random House, 1961.
35. BERT KAPLAN. *A Study of Rorschach Responses in Four Cultures.* Cambridge: Papers of the Peabody Museum, vol. 42, no. 2, 1954; and Gardner Lindzey, *Projective Techniques and Cross-Cultural Research.* New York: Appleton-Century-Crofts, 1961.
36. C. W. M. HART, "The Sons of Turimpi," *American Anthropologist,* 56: 242-261, 1954; Victor Barnouw, *Culture and Personality.* Homewood, Ill.: The Dorsey Press, 1963; J. J. Honigmann, *Culture in Personality.* New York: Harper and Row, 1967.
37. J. O. ELLEFSON, "Personality and the Biological Nature of Man," In Edward Norbeck et al (eds.), op. cit.
38. EDMUND LEACH, 1961, op. cit.
39. EDWARD WINTER, "Beyond the Mountains of the Moon," *The Lives of Four Africans.* Urbana: University of Illinois Press, 1959.
40. ROBERT LOWIE. *The Crow Indians.* Farrar and Rinehart, 1935.
41. A. C. VAN DER LEEDEN, "Social Structure in New Guinea," *Bidragen Tot De taal—Land—En Volkenkunde,* 116: 119-149, 1960.
42. PETER GARDNER, 1966: 409, op. cit.
43. COLIN TURNBULL, 1961, op. cit.
44. ELIZABETH THOMAS, *The Harmless People.* New York: A. A. Knopf, 1959.
45. ROBERT B. EDGERTON, "On the 'Recognition' of Mental Illness," In S. Plog and R. Edgerton (eds.), *Changing Perspectives in Mental Illness,* pp. 49-72, New York: Holt, Rinehart and Winston, 1969.
46. L. L. LANGNESS, *A Day for Stealing* (Unpublished ms.),
47. ROBERT B. EDGERTON, 1969, op. cit.
48. Some useful introductory material can be found in M. E. Goodman, *The Individual in Culture.* Homewood, Ill.: The Dorsey Press, 1967; J. B. Casagrande, *In the Company of Man. Twenty Portraits of Anthropological Informants.* New York: Harper and Brothers, 1960.

49. LEO POSPISIL, "Social Change and Primitive Law: Consequences of a Papuan Legal Case," *American Anthropologist*, 60: 832-837, 1958.

50. GERHARD LINDBLOM, *The Akamba in British East Africa*, Volume 17 (2nd ed.), Uppsala, Archives D'etudes Orientales, 1920.

51. PHILIP NEWMAN, "Wild Man Behavior in a New Guinea Highlands Community," *American Anthropologist*, 66: 1-19, 1964.

52. R. EDGERTON, 1969, op. cit.

53. C. MacANDREW and R. EDGERTON, 1969, op. cit.

54. WALTER GOLDSCHMIDT, *Kambuya's Cattle: The Legacy of an African Herdsman*. Berkeley: University of California Press, 1969.

55. PAUL SPENCER, The Samburu. *A Study of Gerontocracy in a Nomadic Tribe*. Berkeley: University of California Press, 1965.

56. M. J. MEGGITT, 1967, op. cit. p. 255.

57. *ivid.*, p. 259.

58. *ibid.*, p. 259.

59. MARTIN YANG, *A Chinese Village: Taitou, Shantung Province*. New York: Columbia University Press, 1945.

60. MARGERY WOLF, *The House of Lim. A Study of a Chinese Farm Family*. New York: Appleton-Century-Crofts, 1968.

61. J. K. CAMPBELL, *Honour, Family and Patronage. A Study of Institutions and Moral Values in a Greek Mountain Community*. Oxford: Clarendon Press, 1964.

62. ERNESTINE FRIEDL, *Vasilika: A Village in Modern Greece*. New York: Holt, Rinehart and Winston, 1964.

63. ROBERT REDFIELD, 1955, op. cit.

64. AMITAI ETZIONI, *The Active Society. A Theory of Societal and Political Processes*, New York: The Free Press, 1968, p. 625.

65. A. K. COHEN, op. cit., p. 4.

66. For example, see: Walter Goldschmidt, *Comparative Functionalism. An Essay in Anthropological Theory*. Berkeley: University of California Press, 1966; Lionel Tiger and Robin Fox, "The Zoological Perspective of Social Science," *Man*, 1: 75-81, 1966, and the work of many primatologists such as Washburn and DeVore.

67. ALEXANDER THOMAS, STELLA CHESS and HERBERT BIRCH, *Temperament and Behavior Disorders in Children*. New York: New York University Press, 1968.

68. DAVID HUME, *A Treatise of Human Nature*. London; John Noon, 1739.

3

Areté–Motivation and Models
for Behavior

WALTER GOLDSCHMIDT

Professor of Anthropology
Department of Anthropology and
Department of Psychiatry
University of California at Los Angeles

1. *The Concept of Areté*

Once upon a time [Edith Hamilton wrote]—the exact
date cannot be given but it was not far from 450 B.C.—an
Athenian fleet cast anchor near an island in the Aegean as the
sun was setting. Athens was making herself mistress of the
sea and the attack on the island was to begin the next morning. That evening the commander-in-chief, no less a one, the
story goes, than a Pericles himself, sent an invitation to his
second in command to sup with him on the flag-ship. So
there you may see them sitting on the ship's high poop, a
canopy over their heads to keep off the dew. One of the
attendants is a beautiful boy and as he fills the cups Pericles
bethinks him of the poets and quotes a line about the "purple light" upon a fair young cheek. The young general is
critical: It had never seemed to him that the color-adjective
was well chosen. He preferred another poet's use of rosy to

describe the bloom of youth. Pericles on his side objects: that very poet had elsewhere used purple in the same way when speaking of the radiance of young loveliness. So the conversation went on, each man capping the other's quotation with one as apt. The entire talk at the supper table turned on delicate and fanciful points of literary criticism. But nonetheless, when the battle began the next morning, these same men, fighting fiercely and directing wisely, carried the attack on the island (1).

These are leaders of ancient Greece—at once soldiers, poets, philosophers, statesmen. They are Greek gentlemen. They are of the aristocracy. They possessed that quality that the Greeks called *areté*.

Werner Jaeger, in his *Paedeia* (2), develops for us the concept of areté. Let us hear what he has to say about this quality, both for what it meant to the Greeks themselves, and what general meaning it has for the common enterprise of psychiatry and anthropology.

> ... We can find a more natural clue to the history of Greek culture in the history of the idea of *areté*, which goes back to the earliest time. There is no complete equivalent for the word areté in modern English; its oldest meaning is a combination of proud and courtly morality with warlike valor. But the idea of areté is the quintessence of early Greek aristocratic education. ...
> In Homer, as elsewhere, the word areté is frequently used in a wide sense, to describe not only human merit but the excellence of non-human things—the power of the gods, the spirit and speed of noble horses. ... Areté is the real attribute of the nobleman. The Greeks always believed that surpassing strength and prowess were the natural basis of leadership: it was impossible to dissociate leadership and areté. The root of the word is the same as that of αριστος, the word which shows superlative ability and superiority and αριστος was constantly used in the plural to denote nobility. It was natural for

the Greeks, who ranked every man according to his ability, to use the same standard for the world in general. That is why they could apply the word areté to things and beings which were not human, and that is why the content of the word grew richer in later times. (pp. 5-6)

The early form of areté, as used by Homer, relates to a widespread concept among primitive people, for which anthropologists have come to use the Melanesian word *mana*. Mana is the quality of spiritual strength that inheres in an object and gives it superior powers—the arrow that flies straight, the boat that proves itself yare, the man of leadership. It is not unreasonable to assume that in some pre-Homeric time the word had a closely related meaning in Greece. Jaeger continues:

An essential concomitant of areté is honour. In a primitive community it is inseparable from merit and ability. Aristotle has well described it as a natural standard for man's half-realized efforts to attain areté. 'Men,' he says, 'seem to pursue honour in order to assure themselves of their own worth—their areté. They strive to be honoured for it, by men who know them and who are judicious. It is therefore clear that they recognise areté as superior.' The philosophy of later times then bade man obey an inner standard: it taught him to regard honour as the external image of his inner value, reflected in the criticism of his fellows. But the Homeric man estimated his own worth exclusively by the standards of the society to which he belonged. He was a creature of his class: he measured his own areté by the opinion which others held for him. (pp. 8-9)

The concept of areté seems particularly useful to the understanding of both social systems and of individual behavior, and I want in the following to explore it for this potential. You will soon discover that I use this word where

others—myself included—have used the word values, a word
to which I will occasionally turn. But the diverse uses of
this common word have led to confusions—between the ac-
tual and the ideal, between the desirable and the desired,
from its meaning in economics, and from the fuzziness that
naturally inheres in words that are a part of everyday
speech.

We may define areté as the qualities a person should
ideally possess, according to the consensus of his community.
Every normal community has a set of ideas of human conduct we may call its areté. If we are to understand the *work-
ings of society* we must take cognizance of this phenomenon
as it is one of the most important aspects of institutionalized
behavior, though not always given overt expression. If we
are to understand the *character of any particular society*, we
must know what elements of human behavior enter into its
areté, what its particular ideals are. For the central point is
that every people has ideals but the nature of these
ideals varies from one culture to another. If we want to understand the *character of an individual's behavior*, whether
normal or pathological, we must know the context of values
in which he has grown up, for his behavior is meaningful
only as set against the areté of his culture.

2. The Diverse Forms of Areté

In this section I want to show some of the variant forms
that areté can take by excerpting descriptions from various
authors regarding these qualities in diverse cultures. Jaeger
recognized this variable quality when he wrote that: "The
word areté had originally meant warlike prowess; but it is
clear . . . that a later age found no difficulty in transforming
the concept of nobility to suit its own higher ideals, and that
the word itself was to acquire a broader meaning to suit this
developing idea." (p. 8) The first example has reference to
the Banyarwanda, a people of Ruanda, a small now inde-

pendent country in the beautiful mountainous area lying
between the Congo basin and Uganda, though our reference
is to the form the society had prior to Europeanization. The
Ruanda kingdom was sharply divided into social classes
dominated by the tall, graceful and majestic Batutsi (Mututsi in the singular). Cattle was their wealth, and they
ruled through a feudal network of personal vassalage. The
bulk of the population were Hutu, racially as well as socially
distinct; they were the peasants and cultivated the crops.
There was also a class of pygmoid hunting people. Jaques
Maquet, one of the chief ethnographers of the aboriginal
Banyarwanda culture, after noting some specific values, such
as cattle, children, power, and military prowess, writes:

> A Mututsi also greatly desires to be regarded as hav-
> ing *ubugabo*.
> This means the quality of being a man (*mugabo*);
> it includes trust-worthiness in keeping promises, gen-
> erosity in treating one's friends well, liberality towards
> the poor, moral courage in accepting one's responsibili-
> ties. In a society where relations of inferiority and
> superiority are predominantly personal, in the sense
> that authority is rarely abstract (a law, a principle)
> but generally identified with a person (chief, king, lord,
> etc.), emphasis is laid on fidelity in personal relationship.
> Another quality that the Batutsi are extremely
> proud to have is *itonde*. This may be translated as 'self-
> mastery.' To lose one's temper, to manifest violent emo-
> tion by crying is really shameful. Anger, in particular,
> should not be violently expressed. The demeanour of a
> Mututsi should always be dignified, polite, amiable, if
> a little supercilious. Batutsi manners have often been
> called hypocritical. This would be true if such behavior
> were displayed in an extrovert culture where it is con-
> sidered unethical not to express to a person exactly what
> one thinks about him. But in Ruanda it is taken for
> granted that only vulgar persons reveal all their atti-
> tudes and emotions. This is understandable in a strongly

hierarchical society, where the authority of a superior is not restricted to certain specific domains of the life of his inferior, and where to express any disagreement with the superior is thought inappropriate. This is the point of view alike of the inferior (and everyone in Ruanda, except the king, has a superior) and of the superior (and any Mututsi is the superior of a certain number of people) (3) (pp. 178-181).

The Bahutu, the peasant class, does not share these ideals, and are not expected to be self-controlled, though Maquet claims they are impressed by the external dignity of the Batutsi (4). Already we discover something of importance about areté; namely, that it can vary with respect to subcultures within a society, a point of major importance in *our* own native scene.

My next example is from the Omda division of the Humr tribe, Arabic speaking peoples of the Sudan Republic. They are also a stock-keeping people, but they do not have a state organization and social class. Kinship patterns and personal obligation bind the population together, and we see this and the importance of property in the formulation of areté among them from Ian Cunnison's description. (5)

If a man wants wealth—and every man wants wealth—he has to work hard, and he has to pray five times a day. Wealth is everything; it means you can be generous. With generosity you get a name. With a name you get women, and you get a political seat if you like. What more do you want? But cattle, if you have no sheep, are worthless; with a flock you can give your guests meat as well as milk. These men with great herds of cattle are evil men, for no man could have built a herd of a thousand head and have been generous at the same time. If that man were generous, he would have a smaller herd. A man to be happy must have wives to cook for him, and young sons to herd the cattle. Then he is content, he has milk to drink, and plenty of tea.

He may not be a sheikh, but he is a king all the same. He lies under his tree, his sons herd the cattle, his followers do the work of camp, his wives cook and brew tea for him, his cattle low in camp in the evening as they're milked. When he has guests, he catches a ram and throws it to the ground and slaughters it. These are the sweets of life. You've heard what the minstrel has to say?

> They migrate and they low
> They camp and they low
> They give the liquid butter the old men love
> They carry the maidens with jangling bells
> If their owner's a lizard you'll say he's a crocodile
> If his speech is all curses you'll say it is kind
> You owner of land can lie down and rest
> If you have none, go and seek work in the towns.

By God, without cattle a man is nobody. (p. 313)

Cunnison describes the leader among his people by saying:

His fame as son of Omda Merida was justified by his powers as an elephant hunter. His daring, in riding on horseback to decoy the elephant into the ambush of young spears, had brought him a renown among young and old, men and women. He mastered, too, the art of galloping down giraffe: tenaciously to course a giraffe, to gallop over miles of pitted ground, to go into flying hooves, and there to spear it was the mark of a man among the arabs (pp. 311-12).

Another African people, living in what is now Malawi, has a very different notion of what qualities a person should have. The Nyakyusa have some livestock, but live chiefly from their gardens. Monica Wilson (6) has described their culture in detail:

One of the values most constantly stressed by the Nyakyusa is that of *ukwangala* which, in its primary sense, means 'the enjoyment of good company' and, by extension, the mutual aid and sympathy which springs from personal friendship. It implies urbane manners and a friendliness which expresses itself in eating and drinking together; not only merry conversation, but also discussion between equals, which the Nyakyusa regard as the principal form of education. 'It is by conversing with our friends,' said one of our witnesses, 'that we gain wisdom (*amahala*); and it is bad to sit still in men's company. A man who does this is a fool; he learns no wisdom, he has only his own thoughts. . . . It is bad to live alone far from other people, such a man learns nothing: he never learns to express himself well, to converse wittily with friends, or to argue a case with eloquence. It is better to live with other people.'

We are not always given so cogent a description of the dominant values of a culture, but must extract them from aspects of behavior. Among the Ila-speaking people, who live in what is now Zambia, there was again no government beyond the local chief, whose position was dependent upon his personal qualities, as well as his wealth in goods. Succession to such office had to be ratified by a council of elders who, though they took cognizance of rules of succession, were more concerned with personal attributes. They said however, "that the fearsomeness of the ant-hill is the long grass upon it," referring to the fact that it in turn might hide a snake, but making indirect reference to the importance of what one possessed, rather than merely what one was. As in Ruanda, possessions of consequence were cattle. The Ba-Ila also said: "chiefdom is serfdom," for a leader among the Ba-Ila was expected to spend his time in meeting the needs of his people. Other qualities were expressed in the sobriquets addressed to the chiefs and set forth by Smith and Dale (7) in their classic work:

A hunter or warrior may be entitled "the great spiller of blood"; "little-hemp, intoxicator of men," i.e. he can overcome those far greater than himself; "he who does not seek shelter, but stands in a clear space, facing the foe"; "a snake in a bundle of wood," i.e. dangerous; "great weaner of little animals"; "the rinderpest," i.e. destroyer of animals and men; "the famine-breaker," i.e. in famine time he feeds people on the game he kills; "like a great log in transformation," i.e. in ordinary times he can be handled with impunity, but on occasion he flares up like a burning log. Mungaila of Kasenga has these among other titles: "porridge," i.e. cool on top, but hot beneath the surface . . . (pp. 366-367).

We extract from these values of forcefulness, power, controlled action, not wisdom or judgment or dignity or companionship.

The Ba-Ila lived in an area disrupted by wars and invasions that were the secondary consequences of the Zulu wars of the early 19th century. Each tribe lived in an enclosed village and had to be prepared to protect itself against incursions by Ngoni and other marauding groups. Under such circumstances, the virtues they honor are eminently practical. By contrast, the Hopi Indians of the southwest lived huddled in villages, protected by the steep sides of the mesas on which they lived, and eked out a precarious existence by growing maize on small plots. They were thus forced into close collaboration in their workaday life. This situation lies at the base of the gentle values that the Hopi themselves refer to as "the Hopi Way," the major elements of which have been listed by Richard Brandt (8):

The Hopi conception of the ideal man has only a few main themes.

A good family man: is industrious and thrifty, works to provide more material comforts for his family, is concerned for his children and has affection for them, is prudent and cautious.

Agreeable in his social relations: is polite and kind, does not hurt others' feelings, does not get into disputes, does not complain, does not get angry, does not gossip, is not grouchy or mean, heeds valid criticism without taking offense, is cordial, does not cause trouble by having affairs with others' wives.

Not dangerous: he is peaceable, does not get drunk or into brawls.

Cooperative: helps in community enterprises, does what he is asked to do, gives time and effort for the group and especially for relatives, can be counted on for advice, is reliable.

Generous: is generous with his help and food; is sympathetic, hospitable, and unselfish.

Honest: pays his debts, keeps his promises, respects property rights.

Modest: is not a snob but not bashful.

Quiet and unobtrusive: does not try to be important, has no political ambitions.

Cheerful: does not worry, is not vengeful or jealous, maintains his mental equilibrium, is indifferent to unjust criticism.

Manly and brave (but on the submissive side in social relations).

A good worker: is persistent, foresighted, and careful. (p. 138)

Yurok ideals are of a very different kind. The Yurok Indians and their neighbors the Hupa, with whom I did apprentice field work, live in the northwestern corner of California in an area rich in salmon, acorns and wild products, upon which they supported a rather secure life by dint of hard work. They would have found the list of Hopi virtues ridiculous. I have myself summarized some of their qualities (9).

The ethical pattern in Northwest California may be examined under its three fundamental features: the moral demand to work and by extension to the pursuit of gain; the moral demand of self denial; and the individuation of moral responsibility.

There is a strong compulsion to work heavily emphasized in child rearing, supported by the religious beliefs and demands, and expressed as a basic element in behavior. Northwest Californians were a busy and creative people. Wallace writes, "Both a man and his wife are constantly busy. . . . Some seasons of the year are marked by more activity than others, but during none of them is anyone idle for long. The life is one of continuous routine work, although not necessarily of drudgery." Even in pregnancy a woman is expected to work: ". . . if a woman took it easy before she had her baby, the other women figured she was lazy and talked about her." "Old people continue their economic activities as long as possible; only when they become too feeble to endure hard work do they give up."

The second commandment of the Northwest Californians was worldly asceticism. The Yurok was exhorted to abstain from any kind of over-indulgence —eating, sexual gratification, play or sloth. The evidence here is definitive. For instance, sexuality was unclean. The sex act might not be committed in the dwelling house but was performed on the beaches. Youths were exhorted to be continent, and a woman particularly to preserve her virginity until married. Even after marriage, a man was expected to restrain himself: ". . . It's not good to be with a woman all the time. It's bad luck in getting money or hunting deer. A man weans himself from doing that as much as he can. . . . Most men have strong minds and good control . . ." and again, "If a man has too many kids, he is thought to be hoggish, like a dog."

"The third feature . . . is the individuation of moral responsibility. . . . [The individual] was neither the creature of some unseen power nor the product of circumstance, but the master of his own fate." (pp. 513-515)

The proper Yurok and Hupa was tough, hard, self-controlled, and master of his own fate; he brooked no insult and took strong and immediate action against anyone who brought him harm or indignity, which he took in legal encounters which he was prepared to support by physical force. He sought personal wealth, which was the measure of his status, which he pursued relentlessly, at the cost of physical comforts, the appetites, and human sociability. This pursuit had the quality of religious zeal, in that the wealth consisted of the religious paraphernalia that made it possible for him to take a leadership role in the major religious rituals (10). Erikson (11) describes their appetitive restraints both in food and sex, expressed in myths and cautionary tales. Sexuality and gluttony were viewed as sinful, in the true religious sense of the word, though avarice was not.

For my final example I turn to Bateson, (12) who gave such explicit attention to these qualities among the Iatmul, a people of New Guinea. I might note that he, more than any of the other authors quoted, paid attention to the position of women in this context, but we will stay with the masculine side in order not to complicate matters. He also recognizes that there exists more than one masculine model, even though he is describing a small, homogeneous tribal society.

> The natives regard two types of man with approval. The first is the man of violence and the second the man of discretion. Of these, the violent type is the most admired, and such a man is described with enthusiasm as "having no ears." He pays no attention to what is said to restrain him but suddenly and recklessly follows his assertive impulses. . . .
>
> Such men though admired would, I was told, not be trusted with esoteric information, because the natives fear that in the erudite debating about the system of names and totems, such an uncontrolled person may blurt out some important piece of secret lore or provoke a brawl by too rashly exposing his opponents' secrets. Thus with his little knowledge of esoterica, the violent man will behave in debate in the sort of way which I

have described above, filling out his speeches with histrionics and obscene reference.

The more discreet type . . . is the repository of mythological knowledge, and it is he who contributes erudition to the totemic debating and keeps the discussion on more or less systematic lines. His balance and caution enable him to judge whether to expose his opponents' secrets, or merely to indicate by some trifling hint that he knows the secrets, such a hint being tantamount to a threat of exposure. He knows how to sit quietly in the debate carefully watching his opponents to judge whether they really know any of the important secrets of his clan or whether their trifling hints are only a bluff to frighten him into ceding some point.

In mythology these two types are contrasted. There is a series of tales of two brothers of whom the elder, Kamwaimbuangga, was of the discreet type while the younger, Wolindambwi, was a man of violence. Of these it is the latter who is the great hero, but who in fits of temper set fire to the original mythological ceremonial house and killed his sister's son . . . (pp. 161-2).

These examples will suffice to show how variantly the common theme is played as we move from one culture to another. Here a man is expected to be reserved and aloof, there friendly; here a man is respected for his capacity to take violent action, elsewhere he must restrain his impulses in cooperative action, while in a third place, restraint may be valued if it is only a mask for the controlled expression of violence; in one place generosity, in another thrift and the firm expression of self interest, while elsewhere as in the famout Potlatches of the Northwest Coast, the use of giving as an expression of hostility is viewed as the essence of manly behavior.

We cannot demonstrate that areté is a universal feature of human situations, but clearly it is a recurrent feature, and I would argue that its absence would be a kind of social pathology. Indeed the famous description of the people of the island of Dobu by Reo Fortune (13) gives us a picture of what happens in the absence of strong moral commitments.

3. *The Fallacy of Universal Human Values*

The late Abraham Maslow (14) has directed his attention to the problem of values as an element in human motivation. He writes as follows:

> We can certainly now assert that at least a reasonable case has been made for the presence within the human being of a tendency toward, or need for self-actualization, of psychological health or maturation, and specifically as growth toward each and all of the sub-aspects of self-actualization. . . . (p. 125).

I am much in agreement with such a statement, and said much the same thing when I developed the concept of a universal "need for positive affect." (15) But when he proceeds to discuss what these qualities are he is shockingly culture-bound, having no recognition of the diversity of values. He continues:

> . . . the human being has within him a pressure (among other pressures) toward unity of personality, toward seeing the truth rather than being blind, toward being creative, toward being good, and a lot else. That is, the human being is so constructed that he presses toward fuller and fuller being and this means pressing toward what most people would call good values, toward serenity, kindness, courage, knowledge, honesty, love, unselfishness, and goodness. (p. 126)

This error is to be viewed as an extremely serious one, leading into a line of thought that is not merely wrong, not merely counter-productive but actually harmful. It leads to

the fallacy, that any anthropologist must view as arrant
nonsense, such as this by Robert S. Hartman (16).

> *The absoluteness or relativity of value* is an age-old
> question. Its resolution is simple. The question is
> whether there is an absolute norm of value, that is, a
> universal measure in terms of which every other value
> is determined. The answer, as we have seen, is, yes,
> there is. The universal norm of value for each thing is
> the thing's own concept or name. Norm equals name.
> Whenever I judge a thing as to its value, I compare the
> meaning of its name with the properties of the thing
> itself. Just as I can value things, I can value value. The
> concept "value" is defined in formal axiology as we
> just did: the degree of a thing's fulfillment of its con-
> cept. Hence, the value of value is the fulfillment of the
> concept of value; and axiology, as defining this concept,
> is the absolute standard of value. It is based on the
> logic of the human mind itself (p. 123).

The essence of areté lies in a social consensus. It is not
necessarily what is good for the individual; it is not necessarily what he likes, and, unfortunately perhaps, it is not
what he always gets or always does. It is what ought to be
if it weren't for human frailty, circumstantial factors, and
the like. But the ought is a moral imperative that lies within
the minds of a group of persons who recognize some kind
of spiritual unity among themselves, it is transmitted in the
process of socialization and reinforced by institutional devices. Any effort to reduce all forms of areté to some common
denominator will either be a falsification or will result in
such vague generalization as to be meaningless. It is the
particular content of the areté of a particular social group
which is of interest to us, and which must be especially attended by the psychiatrist in his treatment.

We will return to the modes by which values are acquired, but first we must take cognizance of why they should

vary. For though areté takes on different forms, the form it takes in any one community is not entirely arbitrary.

4. The Ecological Factor in the Formation of Areté

Areté is responsive to the circumstances in which a society finds itself—to its ecologic context. The changes that Jaeger found in the Greek areté reflect changes in the circumstances of Greek life from an earlier epoch when the city-states were essentially tribal and warlike to those that existed when they became increasingly urban, individually enriched, and more given to political than military means of handling relationships.

We may illustrate the adaptive character of areté with the classic contrast Ruth Benedict (17) formulated between the Apollonian Pueblo Indians and the Dionesian Northwest Coast and Plains Indians. The Hopi values described by Brandt showed how muted the expressions of personal aggrandizement are. In psychoanalytic terms, the Pueblo child has so early internalized fear of his aggressive impulses that he avoids any kind of competitive relationships to the extent that he cannot even enjoy winning at games—though Benedict, being a very gentle soul, viewed this lack of aggression with approbation. To the Hopi, of course, it is simply The Hopi Way, i.e., it is areté. The Plains Indian has no such repression; he is openly competitive, especially in the physical arena, where as an adult he will be engaged in a continuous pattern of aggressive warfare, compounding his personal glory through raiding enemy horses, killing, maiming, and counting coup—and openly boasting of his exploits years later around the campfire. What situational factors may account for this difference?

Each pattern is necessary to the life modes that the respective environments have placed upon these tribes. We have already noted that Hopi live cramped together, eking out a livelihood through highly cooperative farming; the cooperative mode is essential for survival. Competitiveness cannot successfully be directed toward the outside and it stands as a constant threat to the community as a whole. The child is socialized to the orientation which is reinforced for those about to enter adult life by the community rituals of initiation in the Kivas. (18)

By contrast, the Plains Indian must be socialized to mobilize his competitiveness in order to exploit a mobile resource, the buffalo and other game of the plains, and to protect life and horse (which are their essential capital) against theft and destruction from warlike neighbors. The child is socialized to these orientations, and as he enters manhood he seeks a personal protector for himself through the vision quest. Hear what Erikson (19) has to say about the Dakota Sioux:

> . . . It fell to the older brothers, at this stage, to introduce the small boy to the ethos of the hunter and to make loyalty between brothers the cement of Dakota society. Because of their exclusive association with the boasting older boys, the smaller ones must have become aware early enough of the fact that direct phallic aggressiveness remained equated with the ferocity of the hunter. It was considered proper for a youth to rape any maiden whom he caught outside the areas defined for decent girls; a girl who did not know "her place" was his legitimate prey, and he could boast of the deed.
>
> Every educational device was used to develop in the boy a maximum of self-confidence, first by maternal generosity and assurance, then by fraternal training. He was to become a hunter after game, woman and spirit. The emancipation of the boy from his mother, as well as diffusion of any regressive fixation on her, was accomplished by an extreme emphasis on his right to autonomy and on his duty of initiative. Given boundless trust, and gradually learning (through the impact of shaming rather than through that of inner inhibition) to treat his mother with reticence and extreme respect,

the boy apparently directed all sense of frustration and rage into the chase after game, enemy, and loose women —and against himself, in his search for spiritual power. Of such deeds he was permitted to boast openly, loudly, and publicly, obliging his father to display pride in his superior offspring. One cannot help feeling that the woman was exploited for the sake of the hunter's unbroken "spirit"; and, indeed, it is said that suicides were not uncommon among Sioux women, although unknown among men (pp. 143-144).

I have engaged in an extensive study of the adaptive process in culture, one aspect of which concentrated on the values expressed by the people. Briefly, the research team made an examination of four East African tribes, each of which engaged largely in farming in some sectors of their territory and in pastoralism in others, so that by choosing one community from each we could compare the patterns of behavior and we could discover whether aspects of behavior were consistent within one economic type across tribal boundaries (20).

Robert Edgerton gave a schedule of questions and tests to a sample of over 500 members of these four tribes (21). He found that the personal characteristics of these two populations consistently differed in accordance with economic activity throughout the four tribes, despite the fact that the two sectors shared a common tribal culture, were in close social contact with one another, and often intermarried. Though some elements of personality, behavior and value were consistent within the tribe, he found many that reflected the economic circumstances. The pastoralists, in keeping with the requisite of mobility, valued independence and direct aggression in interpersonal behavior, and demonstrated a syndrome of masculine sexuality not unlike that described for the Sioux by Erikson. The farmers, in keeping with their tendency to live in closed communities, preferred indirect action and the masking of emotional feeling, and did not value masculine aggressivity.

The importance of such findings is that they enable us to say not only that values differ from people to people, but that the values reflect the demands made on the people by the economic circumstances under which they live.

5. The Public Character of Areté

Areté is a public matter; it is shared by a community. The qualities must be given public expression, reiteration, and reinforcement if they are thus to be shared. There are essentially three ways by which the elements entering into the formulation of areté receive public expression.

The first means of communicating areté is in literature, mythology, and sacred texts. The qualities of the culture heroes and the nature of their heroic acts, the morality and cautionary tales that offer models for behavior, the aphorisms which guide conduct are all examples of literature (whether written or oral) expressing elements of areté.

The second method is in ceremony and ritual—particularly initiation rituals. The initiation itself may exemplify the desired traits. The indoctrination to obedience expressed by depersonalized gods in the Kivas (ceremonial chambers) of the Hopi and other Pueblo Indians, performed on a group of youths together, induces conformity. In contrast the "vision quest" of the Sioux and other Plains Indians is an individual act, in which the Indian youth seeks personal power from a guardian spirit, which comes to him through self-inflicted pain and hardship. The Yurok Indian youth's encounter with the spirit world is again different. It is attained while the youth is hard at work in a religious task, gathering firewood of a special kind to be burned in the semi-sacred "sweathouses" where the men get ritual purification. The hardship supports individual power, but is sustained while engaging in a useful activity. In the East African tribe I studied, the Sebei of Uganda, the essence of the initiation was the endurance of the physical pain of late adolescent circumcision and the facing of danger in the form of an impersonated lion, which had to be met with alone and in the dark. The tasks themselves are thus seen to be directly expressive of the qualities that enter into areté in each society. But the elders do not fail to grasp the opportunity of the heightened emotional situation provided by the initiation to verbalize their cultural values for the benefit of the initiates.

The most important public expression of areté is its embodiment in the persons of standing in the community. The personification of the values in individuals who, publicly at least, demonstrate by their prestige and other aspects of their life circumstances the rewards which devolve upon them because they possess areté will inevitably serve as a model for the young. Bateson shows how those who display the virtues of Iatmul manhood in the naven ceremony are honored, and even more pointedly how those who fail to demonstrate them are ridiculed. Whenever people act in response to belief it reinforces the belief itself; when they treat a symbol as real, it reinforces its reality. It is this circularity, this feedback, between symbol and response that is the quintessential character of culture and gives it the power of continuity. Robert Merton (22) called this element the self-fulfilling prophecy. This phenomenon is characteristic of all the interactions that have as an ingredient the existence of a consensus, hence it applies to areté.

6. *The Internalization of Areté*

The social aspects of areté are the center of attention from the anthropological point of view, but they are merely context to the psychiatrist and psychologist. We must therefore divert our attention for the moment to this matter of context and examine the way the individual relates to his social setting. What for the community is a unifying principle of behavior is—or should be—for the individual a lodestone guiding his conduct. For the individual this relates to the discovery of the self, the processes of identification, the formulation of a personal identity, and to what I have elsewhere conceptualized as "the need for positive affect." (23) For the self is to the individual not merely the biological entity which he must feed and comfort and with which he reproduces, but a symbolic entity, with a standing, with an evaluation, with a quality. Jaeger was himself fully aware of this. He wrote: "We must understand the Self is not the physical self, but the ideal which inspires us, the ideal which every nobleman strives to realize in his own life." Like all symbols, as we have already noted, the meaning rests on a consensus, and also on a context. This means that the individual must examine what he is as a social person against the values current in his community. The processes by which this evaluation are achieved are through acceptance by the group (the reciprocal of identification), the esteem which he is accorded by the group, by his ability to command attention and respect from it, and by the material rewards he is accorded.

Unlike the personality or characterological features that have gained the attention of most psychiatrists, the quality of areté is internalized later in life, either during the latency period or in adolescence (or perhaps either, depending on the culture or the individual). The important point is that it is not a set of attitudes laid down in infancy, though what has taken place in these earlier years will have a profound effect on how the individual will handle the cultural values.

Erikson comes to the same conclusion from the opposite end. In his discussion of the epigenesis of identity (24) he finds faith the overriding element in the period of adolescence, saying, "The adolescent looks most fervently for men and ideas to have *faith* in, which means men and ideas in whose service it would seem worthwhile to prove oneself

trustworthy." (128-129, Erikson's emphasis). More directly
to our thesis, he says "The social institution which is the
guardian of identity *is* what we have called *ideology*. One
may see in ideology also the imagery of an aristocracy in its
widest possible sense." (p. 133, Erikson's emphasis). Lidz
(25) is in agreement. He notes that the adolescent's "superego will become modified not only by incorporating new ego
ideals but also through embracing arbitrary but socially accepted standards that are essential to the regulation of any
social system." (317)

Yehudi Cohen (26), concluding his cross-cultural analysis of identity formation, makes the same point when he
says "If there is a point at which personal character is fully
formed and cast into a sociological matrix, this point comes
during adolescence rather than during childhood, even
though the experiences of childhood may establish predis-
positions to later pattern and structure. To put it in clinical
terms, it is during adolescence that the ego is given its basic
and its most lasting contours." (p. 550)

Many societies fix upon the emotional lability of the
pre-puberty (latency) period and the period of adolescence
to dramatize the role the individual is to play in his society
and especially to realign his loyalty and his identification
in relation to that larger group. According to Cohen, pre-
puberty customs which force the child to live outside his
parental house and enforce avoidance between siblings, and
adolescent "puberty rites" have the effect of reinforcing
loyalties to the larger kin group and create what he calls
socialization to interdependence.

While initiation ceremonies offer an ideal setting for the
transmission of values, and are consistently thus used, there
are many other ways that these notions may be reinforced.
Consider the experience Claude Brown (27) describes
by means of which he internalized some dominant ghetto
values:

. . . This was the thing when I was about twelve or thirteen. This was what the gang fights were all about. If somebody messed with your brother, you could just punch him in his mouth, and this was all right. But if anybody was to mess with your sister, you had to really fuck him up—break his leg or stab him in the eye with an ice pick, something vicious.

I suppose the main things were the women in the family and the money. This was something we learned very early. If you went to the store and lost some money or if you let somebody gorilla you out of some money that your mother or your father had given you, you got your ass beaten when you came back home. You couldn't go upstairs and say, "Well, Daddy, that big boy down there took the money that you gave me to buy some cigars." Shit, you didn't have any business letting anybody take your money. You got your ass whipped for that and you were supposed to.

You were supposed to go to war about money. Maybe this was why the cats on the corner were killing each other over a two-dollar crap game or a petty debt. People were always shooting, cutting, or killing somebody over three dollars (p. 265).

He then describes at length how his father forced him to take his beatings rather than run for cover—even when he was being harassed by two much older boys.

The essence of areté is that it relates to the community. This means that it is not merely the father who is responsible for transmitting it to the boy, but the total society. Here again is Claude Brown:

I remember Big Bill, one of the street-corner hustlers before he went to jail for killing a bartender. When I was about seven or eight years old, I remember being on the street and Bill telling me one day, "Sonny Boy, I know you can kick this little boy's ass on 146th Street, and I'll give you a dollar to do it."

I knew I couldn't say no, couldn't be afraid. He was telling all these other men around there on the street that I could beat this boy's ass. There was another man, a numbers hustler, who said, "No. They ain't got no boy here on Eighth Avenue who could beat little Rip's ass on 146th Street."

Bill said, "Sonny Boy, can you do it?" And he'd already promised me the dollar.

I said, "Yeah." I was scared, because I'd seen Rip and heard of him (p. 264).

7. *Areté and Personal Self Interest*

In Freudian terminology, one could say that the internalized areté is the socialization of the superego—its harnessing to the particular need and aims operative under the special circumstances the society finds itself in. Whether or not this is a proper formulation of the situation, it suggests that the motivations that are touched off in response to areté are in conflict with the impulses deriving from other sources of personal satisfaction. Cohen, for instance, fully aware that values are adopted through the process of identification with the group to which the individual is attached, seems to feel that a difficulty derives from the potentiality of overidentification and the lack of individuated action. I would argue, however, that this is not the real problem, that identification tends always to be partial, and that the individual is not only in conflict with his fellow members but is internally conflicted between the ideals of the society and the appetitive behavior deriving from his biological impulses.

When, for instance, we examine the actualities rather than the ideals, we find that the latter are as often honored in the breach in tribal societies as among us. Recalling the demand of submissiveness and cooperation among the Hopi Indians, we find that Brandt (28) notes that "observers of the Hopi have been impressed with the extent of internal strife, and disharmony has been traditional," and that "friction and factionalism are the rule in Hopi political life, both in intervillage and intravillage affairs," and quotes Titiev who says that "the Hopi live in perpetual dread of black magic" (p. 35). And amongst the Sioux and other Plains Indian tribes, with their demands for masculine assertiveness and the separation of the sexes, there is an institutionalized pattern of transvesticism, where men engage in womenly pursuits.

Among the Sebei of Uganda, with whom I have been doing field work, the masculine identification is with the patrilineal kin group, binding together brothers and the progeny of brothers into a unit which is organized for mutual protection and support. Yet brothers show evidence of sibling rivalry and seek to best one another in conflict over their heritage of cattle, and fratricide is fairly common, despite the moral demands of patrilineal solidarity (29).

These observations do not render areté insignificant; rather they point up the recurrent fact that it creates for each individual an inner conflict between the gratification of his biologically based impulses and his socially conditioned personal desires as against those demands which society imposes upon him. For no set of values can fail to place some restraint on personal desire. How the individual will handle this conflict depends on many things; the important point here is merely to recognize that the qualities of areté are never easy to achieve, and that in all societies some men will be possessed of them to a greater extent than others. From the psychiatric point of view it is important to recognize the existence of this conflict as a dynamic element of personal behavior.

8. The Qualities of Areté in Complex Societies

Any shared sentiment, any symbol system, assumes a community of reference. In tribal societies the community is clearly apparent, almost tangible in its character, and relatively homogeneous. The community of reference is nowhere near so clear and cogent in complex societies. With the advent of urbanism five or more millennia ago, social systems came into being in which people lived in mutual interdependence without sharing a common set of values. The earliest known cities exhibit archeological evidence of cultural heterogeneity, with divergent cultural origins, divergent occupations and divergent life styles. The common presupposition necessary to the definition of areté did not exist; conformity had to be imposed by a dominating elite and regulated by codified laws (the earliest of which we have record going back over four millenia). This does not mean that there are no values, but rather that there are different groups each with its own values, including normally, a dominant group which formulates the overriding values to which the others must accommodate, socially and psychologically. That is, the individual in a complex society normally operates in relation to some reference group, from which he receives his primary values. Ethnic communities are the most conspicuous example of this phenomenon, but we have already seen, through Claude Brown's experiences, that this can take place without unified cultural origins. Other self-selected groups may also be defined, as for instance various occupation groups (academicians are certainly a good example) or people with particular life styles, such as special self-selected groups like the "hippies."

Yet in the United States, with its universal demands for a homogenized education and its verbalization of common middle class values emphasizing the Protestant Ethic and the virtues inherent in work, each member of an ethnic minority or a product of ghetto neighborhood is subjected to two divergent value systems. For some ethnic groups, notably the Jews with their strong demand for success and education and the Japanese with their compulsive need for performance, the values of their cultural background and those inculcated by the dominant culture through the schools and other institutions are sufficiently in accord to enable the youth to meet the generic American demand without losing contact with his ethnic values. For other ethnic groups this happy circumstance does not exist. The Italian youth, for instance, is apt to discover that he must make a choice between his ethnic identity and the dominant American values, and finds it difficult to compromise this conflict (31). Herbert Gans (32) has described an urban Inlian peasant-like community in which the local ghetto values take precedence over the middle class values even among youths in school.

A strong sense of ethnic identity may enable an alternate pattern of areté to exist side by side with that of the dominant culture, each accommodating to the other. The same cannot be said for ghetto situations. The slum is not in the same sense an ethnic enclave, but a locality created by the dominant culture for the housing of the poor and the dispossessed. Ghetto values do not spring either from some deep cultural tradition, supported by religion and myth, or from a self-selected group bound by common interests or occupational ties. Elliot Liebow (33) in a study of black men in a Washington, D.C., slum shows how the economic forces prevent men from attaining a satisfactory self-image so that they mythologize their own behavior in what might be called a synthetic areté (34). Though this lacks the reinforcements characteristic of a traditional culture, it nevertheless constitutes an environment against which the individual must measure his own competence, and in terms of which he acquires his self-image. It not only is, but it must be a pattern which is at variance with the areté of dominant society—a counter-culture. It must be thus, for in order to sustain a satisfactory self-image, these men must reject the very basis by which the social hierarchy is legitimatized, i.e., the areté of dominant society (35).

The "value crisis," as everyone knows, extends beyond the slum areas and into a rapidly growing sector of disenchanted middle class youth. The importance of this phenomenon for modern society needs no emphasis here, but some attention should be given to the reasons why it has come into being.

First, there is what may be called the "reality factor"— or in terms of our earlier discussion, the problem of ecological adaptation. The dominant traditional American values are compounded of the Judeo-Christian ethic and the requirements of a frontier existence. Thrift, ingenuity, hard work, and a strong and direct protection of self-interest were necessary elements to the "taming" of the frontiers, and the assiduous application of these virtues brought rewards in personal wealth, comfort and power. But the frontier has long since disappeared, and these virtues are no longer functional in our modern technological society. Just as the atom bomb has rendered warfare (and hence nationalism) obsolete, so too have the pill and penicillin undermined the rationale for premarital chastity, and the existence of surpluses undermined the functions of thrift and hard work. The kind of productive effort which was an absolute necessity to make the frontier habitable is now seen as making that same landscape uninhabitable—perhaps permanently. This situation means that there must be a change in values.

Second, the models of social value in the form of the successful individual embodying and personifying areté is all but lost. For one thing, the rapid technological change renders old knowledge useless, so that the elders (who are the traditional repository of wisdom) have become technologically obsolete. Just as the young engineer knows how to do things his bosses don't understand, so, too, the youth does not find his father an adequate model in the world of everyday affairs, and therefore the chief means by which areté is normally acquired is no longer operative. This situation is exacerbated by the fact that the leaders in modern society, to whom the rewards of prestige, material possessions, and personal comforts are accorded, are with disconcerting frequency demonstrating that they do not possess the virtues which our official doctrine espouses. Instead, we are beset with repeated examples of manipulated images, venality, dishonesty, and the general disregard of established values by those very persons, both in public and in private life, who serve as such exemplars. Whether this is a shift in the nature of leadership or in the information made available in regard to such leadership is, perhaps, a matter of debate. Whichever, the result is the same; namely, the visible fact that the mythic and ideological representation of areté is not personified by those with established status in the society.

9. *Areté and the Psychological Disorders*

Before turning to the importance of the concept of areté to the psychiatrist, it will be well to review the argument of this paper. A set of ideals shared by a community for the proper conduct of its citizenry, which we call areté, is a usual if not entirely universal social phenomenon, but the constituent elements of areté vary from one society to another. These ideals are shared by a culture and communicated in various ways to the young, who treat them as a scale against which to measure themselves as persons. Under normal circumstances, these ideals are internalized and serve as a motivation for action and a basis for restraining the biologically derived impulses during later childhood and adolescence.

In urban societies this simple model is complicated by the coexistence of diverse forms of areté in accordance with the heterogeneity of the population with respect to ethnic origins, occupations, and other reference groups, and there must be an accommodation between these diverse sets of ideals and the overriding areté of the dominant society. These complexities are exacerbated at the present time by the obsolescence of our traditional values in the face of current technological accomplishments and rapid changes in that technology, which render the older person technologically obsolete and thus undermine his normal role as a model for areté, as well as by the venality and corruption in public life. All of this leads to a crisis in values.

There are several points at which this discourse relates to the normal role of the psychiatrist, and I will conclude by making these explicit.

First, the psychiatrist must take cognizance of the existence of values as one attribute of social life, that these values are socially derived, and that their internalization is essential to the formulation of a proper self-image. Second, and more important, is the fact that what constitutes the areté varies from one social group to another, not only between tribal cultures, but between subcultures within our own society, so that in dealing with his patient, the psychiatrist must know the atributes of areté of that patient's reference group. This matter is so central and important that it must be exemplified. For instance, it is as symptomatic of an emotional disorder for a ghetto youth to avoid confrontations and physical combat as it is for a middle class youth to seek out gang warfare. Again, what would seem to be a pathological oedipal fixation in such a middle class youth would be normal behavior for a Mexican boy, who is socialized to a strong and unquestioning attachment to his mother. If the psychiatrist is to understand the implications of what he hears with his third ear, he must take the trouble to learn what the norms of his patient's subculture are, particularly its areté.

Third, within the dominant culture of modern America there is a real crisis in values, which is creating a real and tangible set of problems for middle class youth. The fact that this situation is being played upon by the politicians of the right and the extremists of the left is not directly within the arena of the psychiatrist's competences, but it nevertheless gives dramatic importance to the situation. What is of direct concern to the psychiatrist is that there is a reality factor behind this values crises, that the failure to provide youth with a proper, consistent and meaningful template for behavior deprives him of a means of measuring his own person and therefore of developing a self-image that is meaningful and acceptable. This deprivation is of the gravest importance, for, I would argue, no individual can be healthy and reasonably happy if he cannot find within himself those qualities which he knows are the measure of a man—as that is defined in terms of the society in which he lives.

REFERENCES

1. EDITH HAMILTON, Athenian Values, *The Greek Way.* W. W. Norton & Company, Inc., 1930.
2. WERNER JAEGER, *Paedeia, The Ideals of Greek Culture,* Volume I, *Archaic Greece; the Mind of Athens* (Gilbert Highet, tr.) Oxford University Press, Second edition, 1965.
3. J. J. MAQUET, "The Kingdom of Ruanda," *African Worlds,* Daryll Forde, ed. International African Institute. Oxford University Press, 1954.
4. The Encyclopedia Films has a short motion picture on the life of these peoples which, despite other flaws, demonstrates the remarkable difference in public demeanor of the two classes.
5. IAN CUNNISON, The Omda, *In the Company of Man,* Joseph B. Casagrande, ed. Harper & Brothers, 1960.
6. MONICA WILSON, *Good Company, A Study of Nyakyusa Age Village.* Oxford Press, 1957.
7. EDWIN W. SMITH and ANDREW MURRAY DALE, Etiquette, Chapter XIV, *The Ila-speaking Peoples of Northern Rhodesia.* Macmillan and Co., Limited, 1920.
8. RICHARD B. BRANDT, *Hopi Ethics, A Theoretical Analysis.* University of Chicago Press, 1954.
9. WALTER GOLDSCHMIDT, Ethics and the Structure of Society; An Ethnological Contribution to the Sociology of Knowledge, *American Anthropologist,* 53: 4, 1951.
10. WALTER GOLDSCHMIDT and HAROLD DRIVER, *The Hupa White Deerskin Dance.* The University of California Publication in American Archeology and Ethnology, Vol. 35, No. 8. University of California Press, 1940.
11. ERIK ERIKSON, *Childhood and Society* (Second edition). W. W. Norton and Company, 1963, Chapter 4.
12. GREGORY BATESON, *Naven,* (2nd ed.). Stanford University Press, 1958, Chapter XII. Bateson suggested the study of values, for which he

proposes the word ethology. That word has now taken on another meaning.

13. REO FORTUNE, *The Sorcerers of Dobu: The Social Anthropology of the Dobu Islanders of the Western Pacific.* E. P. Dutton Paperback Edition, 1963. (First Published, 1932.) See also my discussion of this situation in *Comparative Functionalism, An Essay in Anthropological Theory,* University of California Press, 1966, pp. 76-81.
14. ABRAHAM MASLOW, Psychological Data and Value Theory, *New Knowledge in Human Values,* Abraham H. Maslow, ed. Henry Regnery Company, 1970.
15. WALTER GOLDSCHMIDT, *Man's Way; A Preface to the Study of Human Society.* Holt, Rinehart & Winston, 1959, Chapter 1.
16. ROBERT S. HARTMAN, The Science of Value. *New Knowledge in Human Values* (Maslow, ed.). Regnery Company, 1970. (Italics in original.)
17. RUTH BENEDICT, *Patterns of Culture.* Houghton, Mifflin & Co., 1934.
18. Admirably developed in Laura Thompson and Alice Joseph, *The Hopi Way.* University of Chicago Press, 1947.
19. ERIKSON, *op. cit.*
20. W. GOLDSCHMIDT, T. W. PORTER, S. C. OLIVER, F. P. CONNANT, E. W. WINANS, and R. B. EDGERTON, Variation and Adaptability of Culture: A Symposium. *American Anthropologist,* Volume 64, No. 2, April 1965.
21. ROBERT EDGERTON, *The Individual in Cultural Adaptation.* University of California Press, 1971.
22. ROBERT K. MERTON, The Self-Fulfilling Prophecy, *Social Theory and Social Structure* (Revised Edition). The Free Press, 1957, Chapter XI.
23. WALTER GOLDSCHMIDT, *Man's Way; A Preface to the Study of Human Society.* Holt, Rinehart & Winston, 1959, pp. 26-29.
24. ERIK H. ERIKSON, *Identity: Youth in Crisis.* W. W. Norton and Co., 1968.
25. THEODORE LIDZ, *The Person; His Development Throughout the Life Cycle.* Basic Books, 1968.
26. YEHUDI A. COHEN, The Establishment of Identity in a Social Nexus: The Special Case of Initiation Ceremonies and Their Relation to Value and Legal Systems. *American Anthropologist,* Vol. 66, 1964, pp. 529-552. See also his *The Transition from Childhood to Adolescence; Cross-cultural Studies of Initiation Ceremonies, Legal Systems, and Incest Taboos.* Aldine Publishing Co., 1964.
27. CLAUDE BROWN, *Manchild in the Promised Land.* New American Library, 1965.
28. BRANDT, *op. cit.,* p. 35.
29. WALTER GOLDSCHMIDT, *Kambuya's Cattle; The Legacy of an African Herdsman.* University of California Press, 1969.
30. ROBERT LYND, next to Tocqueville, perhaps the most astute observer of the American scene, has described the conflicting values in America. But in very large measure his adumburation of conflicting values

is representative of the conflict between cultural expectations and personal drive. See his *Knowledge for What?* Princeton University Press, 1939.

31. WILLIAM F. WHYTE, *Street Corner Society.* University of Chicago Press, 1965.

32. HERBERT GANS, *The Urban Villages; Group and Class in the Life of Italian-Americans,* The Free Press, 1962.

33. ELLIOT LIEBOW, *Talley's Corner; A Study of Negro Street Corner Men.* Little, Brown & Co., 1967.

34. The issue of whether there is something which may be called "The Culture of Poverty" has been raised both in anthropological and administrative circles. The phrase was coined by Oscar Lewis and picked up by Moynihan (see Charles A. Valentine, *Culture and Poverty; Critique and Counter Proposals,* University of Chicago Press, 1968). We cannot enter here into a discussion of the controversy that has arisen over this, but note only that (1) patterned behavior of ghettos is created by the economic and social deprivation fostered by the dominant society, (2) this creates an environment in which an alternative pattern of values is operative and defines for the local population the nature of ghetto areté and, (3) children growing up in such an environment internalize these values. Thus what has been called the culture of poverty is patterned behavior that comes into being in response to the setting in which poverty exists, and though unsanctioned by tradition and myth, is nonetheless patterned behavior transmitted from generation to generation.

35. I showed a similar pattern of values rejection as the basis for the revivalist religions among the impoverished and socially disenfranchised farm laborers in California agriculture. (*As You Sow,* The Free Press, 1947).

4

System, Symbol and the Image of Man

(Man's Immediate Socio-Ecological World)

LUDWIG VON BERTALANFFY, Ph.D.
State University of New York at Buffalo

In a recent work, Roy Grinker (1967), the well-known psychiatrist and director of Michael Reese Hospital in Chicago, wrote that if there be a third revolution in psychiatry—after the psychoanalytic and behavioristic ones—it would be in the development of general systems theory. Meetings on systems theory at the American Psychiatric Association, many individual researches, recent comprehensive books and reviews (von Bertalanffy, 1968, Buckley, 1968, Gray et al., 1967, Meir, 1969) attest to the interest "systems theory" has received in psychiatry and behavioral science. What is the meaning and significance of this movement?

At a time when miniskirts and maxidresses, long hair, often inarticulate protest and any new fashion or intellectual quirk are hailed as being "revolutionary," the word must be used with extreme caution if it is to be more than an advertising slogan. Fortunately, it can be defined in a technical sense. According to Kuhn's excellent book (1962) a revolution in science is a change when its basic paradigms, categories and models are altered. It is fortunate that Kuhn developed this definition by an analysis of the "scientific revolution" in physics and chemistry of the 16th-19th century, with hardly a reference to recent developments. It is therefore remarkable that the changes with which we are concerned closely correspond with the definition offered.

Before entering into these, another consideration is of some importance. Much is spoken today of the "systems approach" in technology, industry, commerce, defense, politics and other fields. It is generally known that new scientific disciplines and professions have appeared which go under names such as systems analysis, systems engineering, programming and the like, and which were unknown a few years ago. But what first comes to mind when the word "system" is uttered, is nearly everything that is undesirable in the present world. Similar to the early 19th Century Luddites who destroyed machines as the source of their misery and economic suppression, activist students and other discontents protest the "system," although it is often not quite clear whether they mean unpopular professors, the grading of papers, Vietnam, the American society, or the ills of the world in general. No doubt, however, we all suffer, in one way or the other, from the system" whatever this means. This is but a modern term for the eternal problem of the individual and society. The individual is forced into social structures and strictures, family, job, the capitalist economy, the police, the United States, and innumerable others. And the problem became acute in a highly differentiated and mechanized society governed by planning and technological principles, which tends ever more to devaluate the human individual, to convert it into a replaceable part in the leviathan of modern society or into an insignificant wheel of the great megamachine, to use Mumford's expression (1967).

Nevertheless, the conclusion confuses ends and means. Certainly, the systems approach can be used for the further mechanization, enslavement and alienation of man. It was up till now mainly applied to the benefit of the industrial-commercial-military complex, and is only hesitatingly introduced for socially desirable purposes like the stemming of pollution, the planning of cities and the like. But this is not a specific fault of this development. It is part of the ambivalence of every science, technology, and human endeavor. Each can be utilized for beneficial purposes; and is also a potential atom bomb. The second way is usually preferred, unfortunately. All great ideas of man, from the mechanical arts to atomic physics, biological and social science to Christianity and other religions, lend themselves to inhuman purposes; the new trend makes no exception. This rests in man's perversity rather than in Christian dogma, the advance of physics, systems or whatever other target we make responsible as cause of our troubles.

THE ZOOMORPHIC AND THE HUMANISTIC
CONCEPTION OF MAN

The problem posed to the present symposium is a scientific image of man based upon knowledge on the molecular, biological, personality, and socio-cultural levels, from a psychiatric viewpoint.

It can hardly be doubted that the lack of such image is a contributory cause of the crises to which we alluded, and the problems with which psychiatry and mental health are confronted. Former times had their images or ego ideals of man as a Christian, a stoic or British gentleman, a Puritan successful entrepreneur, German humanist, or Marxist class-conscious proletarian. This helped even in times when social and economic problems were much worse than in present affluent society. The modern ideology—that is, science and the world picture it generated—was not yet able to produce an image of man that is satisfactory both in scientific scrutiny and in its value content. Hence what V. Frankl (1969) called the existential vacuum, hippies and flower people, return to a state of the noble savage (who never existed in history, and is possible only on the outskirts of the commercial society he detests), rioters who definitely do not belong to the under-privileged class and can afford revolutionizing because they don't have to earn a living— and likewise all the psychiatrist's concerns with the increase of mental illness, malignant boredom, juvenile gangs and crime, the seeking of an artificial paradise by drug addiction and other manifestations of "sick society."

The "third revolution" to which I alluded essentially means that the paradigms of classical science have become inadequate, particularly in the sciences of man. We are striving toward new paradigms. It appears to me (von Bertalanffy, 1967) they can be subsumed under two focal conceptions. One contrasting to previous "zoomorphic" and reductionist tendencies is a new conception of man trying to define the specifics of human behavior which can be epitomized by the notion of man's *symbolic activities*. The other stands in contrast to the "robot" model of man, which considers the psycho-biological organism essentially as a machine responding to stimuli and governed by utilitarian factors, which latter simulate those of market economy, such as utility, equilibrium, adjustment and the like. In contrast to this is a new paradigm of the psychophysical organism as *a holistic and active system*. Let us briefly outline these paradigms and indicate their significance in psychiatric theory and practice.

Until recently a zoomorphic approach was predominant in psychological experiment, theory and psychopathology. This, of course, means the attempt to explain human behavior in terms of animal behavior, and to reduce it to the latter. Such conception was germane to otherwise different theories and practices.

In the past few decades, zoomorphism has taken several forms. One was the psychoanalytic, with the goal to reduce human behavior to animal "drives," "instincts," or "tissue needs," especially of a sexual nature, to understand it as relaxation of tensions, homeostasis, establishment of a psycho-social equilibrium, or in similar terms. The second was the behavioristic version, in its trend to reduce human behavior to conditioning as studied in laboratory animals, especially the white rat. As A. Koestler (1964) has wittily remarked, it led to the result that the previous, naively anthropomorphic conception of animal and rat behavior was exchanged for a "rattomorphic" picture of human behavior, where human beings appeared as hardly more than rats of a giant size and—what is more—were manipulated in "behavioral engineering" modeled after the conditioning techniques of the animal laboratory and applied in advertising, mass media, political propaganda and education.

We have discussed this elsewhere in some detail (von Bertalanffy, 1967), so let us refer only to the presently most fashionable version of zoomorphism. This is the ethological, i.e. the comparative study of animal behavior and the attempt to resolve the "phenomenon of man" into animal behavior patterns. The prevalence of this way of thinking is demonstrated by the popular success of books like Lorenz' *"Aggression,"* Ardrey's *Territorial Imperative,* Morris' *Naked Ape,* and *Human Zoo,* and others.

Konrad Lorenz, founder of ethological science, was careful to note the "unique position of man," "cultural tradition," etc., but this is hardly the case with his followers. Thus the very human phenomenon of war appears simply as a special case of intraspecific aggression or the Territorial Imperative, man's strange mores as those of a Naked Ape, or feminine inferiority is proved on "biological" grounds (Tiger, 1969).

One may indeed have much fun in arguing whether the territory of the American male for which he has a biological urge to fight actually extends to the jungles of Vietnam and the far side of the moon; or whether the breasts of paleolithic fertility goddesses resemble spherical buttocks to an extent that (according to a theory by Morris) the female bosom developed as a sort of sex-inviting buttocks translocated by a strange way of coition. But apart from such parlor games, the vogue of "zoomorphic" books is a symptom which is quite serious.

It is obvious to the evolutionist and biologist in general that man's digestive, respiratory, sexual, etc., organs are basically the same as those of apes and mammals. So is their functioning, i.e. the physiology of these organs. It is neither surprising, shocking, or a particularly new discovery that the same again applies to behavior, that is, broadly speaking, the neural mechanisms that govern gross or "molar" activities of the species, *Homo sapiens*. We hardly need be reminded of the beastly side of "human nature"—we have seen enough of it in recent history. Consequently, it is important to inventory man's behavioral repertory or his innate "instincts," so as to arrive at a better understanding and—hopefully—control of the *bête humaine*.

It is a different matter, however, to regard man exclusively in the "zoomorphic" way, to consider this as a "nothing-but" explanation, and so to "reduce" man to the animal level. The theory of man as a "mere" animal or Naked Ape founders on the elementary fact that humans have "culture" —articulate language, magic and philosophy, machines and science, swords and atom bombs, cathedrals and department stores and what not—and that animals, apes included, have nothing of the sort. And it is symptomatic of a materialistic and commercial society that "culture" and what it implies tends to be forgotten or even "repressed" in the Freudian sense, in favor of a patently insufficient "model" which "explains" Leonardo's paintings as outflow of an infantile

Oedipal shock, language with all its "meanings" as Pavlovian or Skinnerian conditioning and the web of culture in general as explainable by the *naturalia* found in baboons, antelopes, and cichlid fish.

The first problem of a human psychology, it would therefore appear, is to look for the *differentia specifica* and its roots, irrespective of the extent man shares anatomy, excretion, sexual activities, territorial imperatives or damaging physio-psychological effects of crowding with other primates and mammals. This indeed is the meaning of a naturalistic approach. It has to study communalities or general "laws" of behavior, which is the more important in the human case where much of observable behavior has its often hidden and unexpected, biological roots; but it has equally to study specific characteristics of the individual case. If, according to the best of ethological research, the behavior of different species of geese or coral fish is markedly different, somewhat larger differences are to be expected between white rats, baboons and humans. The ethologist should be the last to presume that rats, roebucks, baboons and men are "all the same." His study of animals is based on minute and careful observation. Only in popular science about man, every- and any wild speculation seems to be permitted and encounters no resistance—the more sensational the better, and with an eye to the fashions of the book market and the amusement of the readers. A review in *The New Yorker*, described as "the author's last attempt to differentiate himself from a ten-spined stickleback," is the best critique I have seen which I cannot resist quoting at some length.

> The thing began when naturalists grew tired of shooting and stuffing the creatures they loved, or pinning them in rows in glass cases, and began peering at them instead in the wild state. . . . Soon there was scarcely a bird, an ape, a gazelle, a dragonfly whose bowings and scrapings, preening, threats, empurplings, and sac-swellings were not being observed somewhere by somebody.

Amid the welter of head-noddings and twig-fiddlings thus brought to light, it was natural that certain resemblances between animal and human behavior should be noted. . . . It had not at this state been suggested that because Horace Walpole decorated Strawberry Hill with colorful Gothic bric-a-brac he was practically indistinguishable from a bower-bird. The differences between man and beast were at first apparent even to the animal-behavior observers, or ethologists, who were at pains to remind their readers that animals were not human. "Let us have none of this anthropomorphism!" . . . As recently as 1953, Tinbergen was writing, "It is scarcely necessary to stress the differences in type of organization between human societies and those of gulls."

It is highly necessary now. Scarcely had these ethologists finished shaking their fingers at sentimentalists who spoke of animals as though they were men when they themselves set to work to prove that men were animals. . . . .

After narrating how, following the ethologists' example, Mr. Ellis set up a tent in Hyde Park for studying the behavior of the human animals, and encountered a London bobby's wrath, he concludes:

He (the policeman) turned so extraordinary a color round the neck that a less objective observer might have supposed he was ready to mate. But I have been long enough at the game to recognize aggression when I see it, whether in stickleback or man. We now had an almost perfect setup for a demonstration of the territorial imperative. The blind was my territory, and so long as I was in it I *must* be the dominant individual. The policeman, however, had pretty obviously never read Mr. Ardrey, so I took to my heels. This proves, I think, that I am less of a chacma baboon than some other ethologists I could name. (Ellis, 1968).

Thus recognition and investigation of human singularity are impending tasks in psychology and psychiatry which were hampered by the zoomorphic and reductionist trends in previous theoretical systems. This, one might presume, is the meaning of "humanistic psychology" often mentioned in recent years. Without entering details which would far surpass the present discussion, it may be submitted that the specificity of human behavior can be described by his symbolic activities. This came to attention only in recent years; not even the term "symbol" is found in many current textbooks. It is apparent that the definition of human behavior in terms of symbolism is preferable to former ones such as language, reason ("Homo sapiens"), use of tools ("Homo faber"), etc. In fact, it may seriously be doubted whether man deserves the designation of Homo sapiens, a being determined by intelligence or foresight; but in all his glories and follies, man is an *animal symbolicum* whose actions are determined by symbolic superstructures he created.

REDUCTIONISM AND SYSTEM

Exploration of symbolism as basis of human behavior was undertaken by the author (e.g. von Bertalanffy, 1965, 1967) and others. We must leave it with the mere statement of the problem and proceed to another paradigm developing in recent science, and its impact on our problem.

The system approach, mentioned in the beginning, emerged from the complexities encountered in science and technology with their progress from simple to ever more complex entities and problems. The classical method of science—indicated at its very start by Galileo with his term of *metodo resolutivo*—was to split up, as it were, complex phenomena into their elementary components or units, to find out the laws governing the latter, and to understand the complex from the elementary parts, units and laws. This is what is conventionally named "mechanistic" science. This approach was essentially similar, and equally effective, in the spectrum of the different disciplines. Physics and chemistry resolved matter and events into ever smaller units, molecules, atoms, elementary particles like protons, electrons, neutrons and others, and learned to understand "macro events" in terms of the composing units and their laws. Biology, in similar fashion, resolved the living organism and its behavior into elementary units such as cells and eventually physical and chemical processes, and the triumphs of molecular biology as well as of medicine are the success story of this approach or methodology. In the same vein psychology searched for "psychological atoms," and found them in elementary sensations or reactions, composition of which would lead to understanding psychology and behavior. Last but not least, technology followed the same way and constructed ever more sophisticated machines out of simple parts or elementary machines—wheels, levers, wedges—which were known since the dawn of civilization and not essentially surpassed until the beginnings of the "industrial revolution." The history of science and technology is the record and successes of the Galilean method.

Slowly, however, it appeared that something was left out in this impressive and amazing success. When it comes to complex entities or "systems," the interactions between many parts become a problem. You have to know not only the "parts" into which the system can be analyzed, but also the "relations" or "interactions" between them. These indeed make the system into a whole which, as a rule, cannot be understood by summation of its isolated parts or, as the saying goes, is more than the sum of its parts. So far as more than random or statistical phenomena are concerned, you will find a characteristic "order" or relations of parts or "laws of organization." Such "system principles" have to be studied in their own right, and are not simply reducible to or obtainable from the laws governing the components when these are taken apart and considered in isolation. It further turns out that such "system principles" are of a general nature and can be studied in an abstract way, independent of the particular nature of the system, its components and the relations or "forces" playing among them. Therefore a "general system theory" is possible and necessary, that is, a doctrine concerned with the general or formal characteristics of "laws" of "systems" (defined as sets of components in interaction) or, in somewhat different terms, general principles of organization and models of systems, irrespective of the nature of elements and the specific forces in the individual case. As it turns out, a theory of systems can be elaborated in various ways; general system theory in the narrower sense (or dynamic system theory), cybernetics, network, compartment, information theory and others are different formulations and approaches toward a general theory of systems (cf. von Bertalanffy, 1968).

Again, this development is structurally similar (or "isomorphic," as the technical term says) in the diverse disciplines. Technology was able to construct fantastic mechanical, heat, electric machines, etc., but when it comes to rocket systems, moon landings, or the complex problems of pollution, one has to consider "the system," and to call on the systems engineer and his computers. Quite similarly in the sciences. The present problems of particle physics appear essentially to be in complex interactions which require novel mathematical approaches. The biologist is concerned not only with units, cells with their amazing structures as revealed by electron microscopy or even the units of molecular biology, DNA and the genetic code, which carries information for the synthesis of species-specific proteins; he wants to know about the "system" or organization: how myriads of physical and enzymatic processes are so coordinated as, in general, to maintain the "system" in continuous exchange of components, how cells differentiate into multicellular organisms with manifold tissues and their diversified functions, how the genetic code, in one case,

produces a bacterium, in others a rabbit or a human, how
the nervous system works, and how all this materialized in
the course of evolution. These and many others are "system
problems." Psychology, again, realizes since the days of
gestalt theory that psychological, behavioral and psychiatric
phenomena are not a "mere sum of parts" but obey laws of
the whole, of organization or "system."

Here we came back to our initial problem. The mechanistic approach was expressed in the machine conception of the
organism in biology, and the "robot model" in psychology,
behavior and psychopathology.

OVERCOMING THE ROBOT MODEL

Basic for the interpretation of animal and human behavior was the stimulus-response scheme, or as we may also
call it, the doctrine of primary reactivity of the psycho-
physical organism. The basis of behavior is supposedly
reaction to outside influences or stimuli present and past.
Again, this was a very general notion germane to otherwise
different or conflicting theories. It is the basic model in
behaviorism, in both versions as Pavlovian or classic, and
Skinnerian or operant conditioning. It is also basic in psychoanalysis insofar as behavior appears determined by early
childhood experience, and the purpose of the "mental ap-
paratus" is to restore psychophysical equilibrium after it
had been disturbed by stimuli (Freud's "principle of equilibrium"). Essentially the same model is at the basis of the
conception of the brain as an electronic computer, and of
the reduction of behavior into feedback circuits. Speaking in
general terms, this is an expression of the other- or outer-
directedness of modern man which Riesman has described;
with the implication that the individual, by way of conditioning, mass media, advertising, propaganda ever more be
made into a robot reacting in ways demanded by the wire-
pullers in a commercial society.

Among the characteristics of the stimulus-response (S-R) scheme is environmentalism, i.e. the notion that the human individual is more or less a *tabula rasa,* his personality shaped by early childhood experience or conditioning, Pavlovian and Skinnerian. Hence follows, intra-specifically (i.e. within the human species), egalitarianism, that is, individual differences are more or less negligible and personality is—and should be—molded by proper child rearing and conditioning; interspecifically, zoomorphism as already discussed, that is the notion that there is not much difference in behavior and its laws of monkeys, cats, rats and humans. The robot model or principle of reactivity further entails the equilibrium theory of behavior; every stimulus is a disturbance of equilibrium, response is its re-establishment. Behavior therefore is homeostasis, gratification of needs or relaxation of tensions. This, in turn, implies the essentially utilitarian nature of all behavior; it is governed by the economic principle of reaching the goal of maintenance with minimum expense.

We shall not attempt a detailed critique of the "robot model" on the basis of psychological experiments and theory which we discussed elsewhere (von Bertalanffy, 1967) but limit ourselves to a brief remark.

I have said previously that modern psychotechniques and behavioral engineering amount to a "functional decerebralization," that is, higher cerebral centers and faculties are superseded by the ruthless conditioning to which modern man is submitted in the incessant impact of mass media, advertising, propaganda, if not doping by drugs.

It now appears to me that even rats and mice suffer "functional decerebralization" under the standard conditions of the psychological laboratory.

Apparently we must completely restructure prevalent views and theory even of animal behavior as they developed over the past fifty years. The behavior of an animal like a mouse or rat, we had been told by learning theory, is built up in a slow conditioning process, by way of trials at random reinforced by reward or punishment. Learning, even under absurdly simple conditions such as the Skinner box or T-maze (or correspondingly, learning of nonsense syllables or by teaching machines), therefore takes scores of repetitions and corresponding time for every step, resulting in a learning curve whose mathematical features and interpretation were endlessly debated.

But take, for example, a recent study (Kavanau, 1969) on captive white-footed mice. They were placed in a vertical maze, 96 meters long with 1205 90° turns, and openings into 445 blind alleys which occupied 53 per cent of the total space. The mice learned to traverse the system in a few days with no reward being given and no prior deprivation; moreover the mice had to learn the maze in both the forward and backward directions because there was only one point of entrance and exit. Similarly it was found that mice avoid activities not initiated by themselves, even activities they engage in when they can do so of their own "volition"; and they resist being forced to stop such activity.

Such observations (and many others to the same effect) seem to allow only one conclusion. Animals in their natural conditions not only command "psychological" mechanisms widely surpassing our own (such as the echo "radar" of bats, the navigation of migrating birds or the "feel" of a parasitic wasp where to inject venom in a caterpillar to immobilize it and prepare it as food for its progeny); even processes believed to be explained "scientifically," turn out to be of an entirely different nature. Animal experiments like those quoted parallel, of course, cognizance of the fact that human learning (e.g. in the teaching process) essentially does not follow the scheme of conditioning by deprivation and reinforcement but takes place by insight into "meaning" without laborious trial and error, "drives" and rewards.

In other words: the whole structure of behavioristic

learning theory, erected over fifty years in innumerable experiments, turns out to be a laboratory artifact valid only for conditions—the Skinner box, the learning of nonsense syllables—where the subject is artificially stupefied by conditions alien to its natural state and environment, to which it is not adapted, and necessarily must react like a machine or moron; behavior under natural conditions for which the animal (or human) carries an innate behavioral repertoire to deal with, follows completely different rules.

The consequence for human behavior is apparent. Not only, as is increasingly realized (Presley, Ausubel, Bruner and others), does the learning process in education not follow the conditioning scheme, so raising questions too on mechanized learning and teaching machines; but even more, conditioning techniques "de-rattisize" a rat, that is, reduce it from an animal fit to cope with and to survive in its natural environment to a moronic reacting machine which could not survive except when provided with food and shelter by the experimenter. Equally, conditioning techniques applied to humans necessarily reduce humans to robots fit for "consumer behavior" imposed by "behavioral engineering," but leaving them empty, dissatisfied and unhappy.

In the present context, another consideration appears important, namely, that modern society is a grand-scale experiment refuting the "robot theory" of behavior and its practical applications.

It appears that modern society shows, almost with the precision of a scientific experiment, that something is basically wrong with the picture of man as drawn by conventional theory. According to this, mental health should be assured when biological needs are granted, hunger and sex are gratified, education does not impose on the child exaggerated scholastic and behavioral demands, and so forth. These conditions were fulfilled in the affluent part of our society with high living standards, new sexual "morality," increasing leisure compared to labor formerly enforced by social conditions, and so forth. What was the result? Instead of mental health, these conditions have led to an unforeseen increase in mental disorders, and even to new forms of mental disease such as existential or noogenic neurosis (Frankl), arising from the meaninglessness of life or existential vacuum; not to mention again the various forms of moral and social decay arising not from need or authoritarian mental trauma in education, but rather in affluence of the "middle" or "upper middle" classes, and in a permissive society.

It may, and has been said that the increase of mental disorders is a consequence of the "stress" of modern life, as is certainly true in some cases. But as a general explanation, it is nearly certainly false. The last war in Europe imposed a stress comparable to all juvenile, matrimonial, business, and race worries of today's America. Indeed, it caused the physiological stress of starvation and undernutrition over many years, added to the psychological stress of continuous menace to life, political suppression at an unprecedented scale, loss of elementary freedoms, etc. But under these conditions neuroses receded, psychoses (schizophrenia) apparently even improved, and there were no crime waves—this being true for both camps, England and Germany. Of course, this is not a recommendation of world wars and dictatorships, but it is a persuasive argument that conventional theory is wrong or insufficient; particularly so in the aspects discussed, the neglect of "higher," specifically human values and the robot model of behavior.

It appears, in fact, that recent developments in psychology are, quite generally, characterized by the revision of these ideas and the advance of a "systems" approach, whether or not their authors explicitly subscribe to general system theory. Discussion would amount to a review of a large part of contemporary psychology and psychiatry ranging from perception (e.g. Gibson's *The Senses Considered as Perceptual Systems*, 1966, Pribram's holograph model) to developmental psychology (Werner, Piaget), to educational psychology (Bruner, Ausubel) to therapeutic approaches (ego psychology, Rogers) to self realization and "being cognitive" (Maslow)—citing only a few names to indicate the general trend, and omitting many others which deserve equal mention. A large amount of modern psychology and psychiatry is "system-theoretical." Present research and theory in psychology (and psychiatry) is scattered, uncoordinated and idiosyncratic of the individual researcher or school so that there is no "theoretical psychology" in any generally agreed sense. It appears that general systems theory may provide a framework of well-defined notions and models by which eventually an integration of the multitude of present approaches and theories into a specific psychology can be attained.

More specifically, the model of the robot or reactive machine has to be replaced by that of the internally active, psycho-physical organism. This activity manifests itself at all levels and both in the cognitive or input, and in the action or output aspect. Cognition is not a passive reception of stimuli or a sort of photographic copy of an outside reality. Rather, the organism creates the world it perceives, conceives and lives in. On the other hand, behavior from primitive automatic motion to play and exploration in animals and children, up to the highest achievements of culture is not a reaction to outside stimuli reinforced by award or punishment, but is expression of immanent activity and, in the last resort, of living creativity.

The system concept is, of course, not a new invention. Precursors go back to Gestalt theory, to organismic psychiatrists like Goldstein and Adolph Meyer, eventually to philosophies like Leibniz' and others. It can be said, however, that only now the preconditions are given to scientifically develop this paradigm, by way of new mathematical approaches, a new epistemology, a change in world view in general.

This is what we take to be the "third revolution" referred to at the beginning. Put into somewhat different terms, the previous mechanistic view which knew only one-way causality and statistical chance events was expanded into a more comprehensive scheme of multivariable interaction and organization. Or, in still other terms: as commonly happens in scientific revolutions, aspects of reality previously suppressed are progressively brought into the field of scientific thought. Not long ago, what characterizes life—wholeness, organization, goal-directedness, purposiveness and the like —appeared as unscientific and metaphysical notions. Now models, theories, mathematical techniques to handle them are elaborated. This is the so-called modern revolution in science and natural philosophy.

To summarize these considerations, the image of man now emerging focuses, first, in contrast to previous zoomorphism and reductionism, on the *specifics of human behavior*: this may be epitomized by the notion of symbolism. Secondly, the previous picture was mechanistic-behavioristic-commercialistic. That is, the general paradigm was that of the machine or robot, its functioning governed by utilitarian factors simulating those of market economy, such as utility, equilibrium, adjustment and the like. In contrast is the *paradigm of the psycho-physical organism as a holistic and active system*. Let us try to enumerate a few consequences that follow from the considerations in which we indulged.

THE PROBLEM OF SCHIZOPHRENIA

The mechanistic view saw the universe as a play of atoms and, at higher levels, as a chance product of genes, cells, reflexes, learning processes and so on. The system view sees an enormous *hierarchic organization*, with specific laws to be detected at each of them.

In psychiatry, the notion of levels has to be taken seriously both in etiology and therapy. This alone will save us from simplistic "nothing-but" theories which always are devastating, and particularly so in complex problems like that of mental disease.

Let us cite, as an example, the present status of *schizophrenia* research and the multitude of hypotheses offered in this field. It is plausible enough that a biochemical or genetic disturbance is at the ultimate root of schizophrenia although, after so many attempts gone wrong, I am not so sure what we actually know in this respect. After having followed these investigations for some twenty years, it seems to me that some progress was made with respect to biochemical bases of emotional components of psychosis, particularly in the elucidation of the epinephrine mechanism. However, even if a biochemical disturbance were indubitably established, it is difficult to see what connection there is with the classical symptoms of schizophrenia, such as the disturbance of thought processes. This problem is of course connected with that of hallucinogenic drugs and the structural similarities of psychotropic drugs with brain-active substances. But in the hope of elucidating schizophrenia by way of experimental "model psychoses," the additional problem appears whether drug-induced states are comparable to clinical psychosis, or are to be ranged as toxic psychoses.

At the next higher level, it is easy to imagine schizophrenic phenomena as a sort of "crossed wires" in neural connections, or even to design some abstract model. But again, our ignorance is profound. We simply do not know what is the neurophysiological correlate of thought (symbolic) processes, and to what extent models like the McCulloch neuron nets correspond to reality. In contradistinction to neuronal theories, we also have safe indices that the brain works as a functional whole. In localized traumas, such as cortical lesions, the ensuing effect is impairment of the total action system, particularly with respect to higher and more demanding functions, rather than disappearance of individual functions; conversely, the system has considerable regulative capacities. So there is a still unreconciled opposition of meristic brain function (as shown in Penfield's experiments of resuscitation of individual memory traces by local stimulation) and its holistic aspects (as demonstrated by the experiments of Lashley, Bethe and others, and clinical experience like that of Goldstein).

At a still higher level, schizophrenia certainly is a symbolic disturbance, an aspect to which we shall return. Again higher up are social (family) relationships such as in Bateson's double-bind hypothesis of schizophrenia. Possibly still higher socio-cultural systems have to be taken into account. The recent increase in schizophrenia may have something to do with the other-directedness and manipulation of man in modern society.

It is beyond the scope of this paper and of the author's competence to evaluate the various hypotheses and respective evidence. I only wish to re-emphasize that apparently various levels and their interactions have to be considered in the schizophrenia problem; or, what amounts to the same, that a multi-disciplinary approach is necessary. A similar hierarchy applies to therapeutic measures, and this corresponds to the present preference of combined therapies such as drug therapy, individual psychotherapy, family and group therapy, community programs, etc. Here is a place where systems theory can give a theoretical framework and even practicable suggestions for therapeutic measures.

Whatever the biochemical bases and the relations to drug-induced model psychoses, we cannot lose sight of the fact that schizophrenia is essentially a disturbance at the symbolic level, and hence a specifically human disease. One cannot very well consider oneself as being Christ or the Emperor of China or being persecuted by the secret police without having ideas of what this means to start with. In the words of Arieti (1965), "severe anxiety reactions, schizophrenia, paranoid states, have very little to do with hunger, thirst, sex per se, but very much to do with conflicts arising from the complicated conceptual world of man." This obviously is unassailable—except for the remarkable fact that psychiatrists were often so blinded by psycho-analysis or biochemistry as not to see the obvious. Arieti (1959) and others have deeply explored schizophrenic thought. I only wish to present a few thoughts arising in the context of systems theory.

One is that schizophrenia is essentially a disturbance of system functions of the experiencing ego. For this reason, individual symptoms do not define the disease (cf. von Bertalanffy, 1960). Consider the classical symptoms of schizophrenia. There is, according to Eugen Bleuler's classical definition, "loosening of associational structure" and "unbridled chains of associations." But it is easy to find examples exactly comparable to schizophrenic thought and speech, for example in "purple" poetry and in rhetoric. "Auditory hallucinations" form an important part of the schizophrenic picture; but exactly similar hallucinations or voices told Joan of Arc to liberate France. "Piercing sensations" are often experienced by schizophrenic patients; but a great mystic like St. Teresa reported identical experience—witness Bernini's statue in Stn. Maria Vittoria in Rome. "Fantastic world constructions" are still another part of schizophrenic disturbance, but we may justly say that the constructions of science widely surpass those of a schizophrenic. The idea that we all travel with inconceivable speed through space, or that matter like a table or my own body mostly consists of empty space, is more fantastic than any schizophrenic world system—except for the fact that it is "true" within the conceptual framework of science.

Such considerations apply to the levels both of perception and concepts. The schizophrenic vision is characterized by illusions, delusions and hallucinations, i.e., as is commonly said, it is "a product of their brains." But the same applies to normal perception. Hallucinations are present even in the healthy individual, at least in dreams. Against the "copy theory" of perception I mentioned, we ever more realize perception to be an active process or a "product of our brains." What we term illusion in the psychological experiment plays an important role in normal vision because it is a basis of constancy phenomena without which a consistent world image would be impossible. And how much of our experience is delusional hardly needs emphasis in view of the distortions of reality imposed by emotional factors, politics and the like.

The contrast of normality with schizophrenia is therefore not that normal perception is a plain mirror of reality "as is," but that in schizophrenia subjective elements run wild and are disintegrated.

A similar consideration, as already said, applies at the conceptual or symbolic level. This is not to say that science is a schizophrenic fancy, nor to identify genius with madness. But the point rather is that not isolable symptoms or criteria but integration makes for the difference. Whether an individual is judged to be and experiences himself as mentally sound or not is ultimately determined by whether he has *an integrated universe consistent within a given cultural framework.* So far as I can see, this criterion comprises all psycho-pathology as compared with normalcy.

I have just introduced the term, "cultural framework" which emphasizes another dimension or aspect of those symbolic activities we consider fundamental for the human mind. Of course, primitive people have world pictures widely different from ours and appearing fantastic to us—paleologic, anthropomorphic, mythical, magical and so forth, as Arieti (1965) has vividly described. Nevertheless, we do not call them mad or schizophrenic. What is the difference? Precisely what I have said: that these world pictures, strange as they may be, are consistent within a given cultural framework and, for this reason, are viable. For this reason, e.g. the magical world of primitives persisted through several hundred thousand years of human evolution and prehistory. It helped through the struggle for existence in an adverse nature and so demonstrated its adaptiveness. Moreover, it created achievements which, with all scientific techniques, we are not able to duplicate: our cultivated plants and domestic animals are still those which were bred by our forebears in the neolithic or agricultural revolution, and hardly an addition was made in the subsequent time, or with modern scientific techniques. The schizophrenic's views, on the other hand, are not within our cultural framework— and this is precisely the reason that we put him into a mental institution.

The same applies to the culture dependence of mental disease in symptoms and epidemiology as studied by Opler (1956) and others. Suffice it to refer to Ruth Benedict's *Patterns of Culture* (1934), for example, to her Kwakiutl Indians. In their potlatch feasts they behaved in a way we would term (and certify) megalomanic, but this was considered normal "in their cultural framework." The same, of course, would apply to the potlatch of American luxury consumption, planned obsolescence, pollution of environment, etc., when envisaged from the viewpoint of a culture more mature and not engrossed in economic schizophrenia.

MIND AND BODY—A NEW APPROACH

This has still wider, philosophical connotations. As we know, one important symptom of schizophrenia is called "loosening or breakdown of the ego boundary." If we accept the "copy theory" of perception, this is a paradoxical and even completely unexplainable phenomenon. If our eyes and brain produce an image of the outer world like a camera does—how can it happen that the boundary between camera and world, object and subject becomes blurred, or breaks down altogether? The paradox is resolved in developmental psychology.

In the child, experience starts with a "primitive adualism" according to Piaget's term. Out of this crystallize, as it were, the two opposites of the world outside and the ego or self. This is a very complex process which was described, in somewhat different terms, by Freud, Piaget, Werner, Schachtel and others. But, in principle, it is generally agreed that there is a process of objectification by which gradually perception of the outside world and the conscious ego are established and separated. Self-evident and convincing as the opposition is between things outside—desks and tables, mountains and stars, electrons and galaxies—and my own perceiving, thinking, feeling self, to us adult Europeans, nevertheless it is not primal datum, but is rather the result of a long development from baby to adult, from primitive peoples to the modern Westerner; and the factors and stages of this development are tolerably well known.

The schizophrenic, on the other hand, regresses to a primitive, partly adualistic, mythical or magical universe which partly resembles that of the child. Again, what makes the difference is the system aspect. Once more, I may quote Arieti (1959) to show the identity of the clinical picture with the concepts of systems theory. The schizophrenic, Arieti says, will "regress to, but not integrate at, a lower level; he will remain disorganized."

Regression, therefore, is not return to an infantile state. Rather it is disintegration of the personality system, de-differentiation and decentralization (Menninger, 1963). De-differentiation means that there is not a loss of individual functions, but a reappearance of primitive states. This is manifest in well-known symptoms of schizophrenia, such as synesthaesia, syncretism, paleological thinking and the like. Decentralization manifests itself in what has been called functional dysencephalization, that is, splitting of personality or, in milder form, neurotic complexes, disturbed ego function, weak ego, etc., which all indicate loosening of the hierarchic mental organization.

Thus the boundary of the ego is both fundamental and precarious. It is slowly established in evolution, child development and human history, and is never complete. It originates in the opposition of exteroceptive senses and proprioceptive experience. But we may confidently say that self identity is not complete before the I and the it, the self and things outside, are named, i.e., before symbolic functions enter.

Schizophrenia shows the paradox that the ego boundary is at once too fluid and too rigid. On the one hand, the insecurity of the ego boundary is manifest in syncretic perception, animistic feelings, delusions, hallucinations and the like. Similarly, at the conceptual level the normal separation is disturbed between outside objects, self, and conceptual stand-ins or symbols for objects. This is what has been variously called "concretistic inability to symbolize," "loss of symbolic capacity" or similar terms. Reification of concepts, i.e. making mental images into real things, is a further characteristic of schizophrenia; hence hallucinations of demons or persecuting police become a menacing reality to the schizophrenic. Another aspect is overemphasis on logical or rational functions. It was said, I believe correctly, that the schizophrenic is the supreme rationalist, as was expressed by K. Chesterton:

> Great rationalists are not rarely mentally ill, and mentally ill, as a rule, are great rationalists. . . . Whoever enters a discussion with a schizophrenic, probably will come out second best . . . for the schizophrenic is not impeded by any considerations of humor, of love, of his own life experience. The schizophrenic is not an individual who has lost his reason; rather he has lost everything except reason. . . . The strongest and most unmistakable characteristic of schizophrenia is the unison of faultless logic and mental contraction. . . . (cited after Friedell, 1927, p. 462).

The same idea applies to society, and particularly our own, with highest rationality in means, i.e. science and technology, together with complete irrationality of goals, e.g. in the armament race in which every participant well knows it is suicidal. Already Marcuse has spoken of the "insane aspects of rationality."

Because the schizophrenic makes up a world of his own creation, he is living as if in a self-created shell, as has been said. In the idiom of system theory, the normal person is an open system with respect to information received from outside, but the schizophrenic ever more becomes a closed system. To use still another term, this is the alienation of the schizophrenic—an ultimate pathological extreme of the encapsulation of personality which we all, more or less, are suffering. The "normal" person open to the world; the encapsulation of the specialist in his business, job, or science permitting him to see only a thin slice of the world; the neurotic dominated by his complexes; finally the schizophrenic with his fantastic self-created world—these are gradations in a spectrum of personality from open to closed system (Royce, 1964).

As already intimated, we approach in these considerations one of the major problems of philosophy. This is the ancient problem of the relation of body and mind. It is not a merely academic problem; rather, it is demonstrated by the "neuropsychiatric split" in theory and practice. If, for example, opening the patient's skull and performing lobotomy, on the one hand, and the soft talk of the psychotherapist on the other are both considered legitimate psychiatric practice, then obviously the question of how the body works on the mind and the mind on the body, becomes an urgent one. Psychosomatic medicine similarly stresses the mind-body relations.

I myself tried to find a new answer to the ancient problem (1964, 1966) and although you will not expect me to give, in a few minutes, a fair presentation of a problem which has worried philosophers for some 2,000 years, I may enumerate a few questions particularly in their relation to psychiatry.

The first is the question of "phenomenological" psychology, that is, of direct or immediate experience. We find in our experience a world around us with all sorts of things or objects and on the other hand, a self or I, who is the experiencer or subject. To give a quick and therefore insufficient and not unobjectionable answer: the distinction of things and self is, as we have heard, based on the grouping or rather the organization of perceptions of the distal senses —visual, tactile—on the one hand, and proprioceptive perceptions on the other. This distinction is not a primal datum or simply "given"; rather it develops in the child and similarly in culture and history. It is not a simple matter of information received from outside, but is closely connected with conceptualization, symbols, verbalization. And there are all sorts of intermediates between objects outside and the perceiving self even in the normal case, but particularly in pathology like schizophrenia, drug-induced states, etc.

The second question is metaphysical. There are apparently two different realities: "matter" in space, and my thinking, feeling, willing "mind." This is the dualism of what Descartes called *res extensa* and *res cogitans*—the "substance extended in space" and the "thinking substance." This Cartesian dualism does not refer to direct experience or the immediately "given"; rather, matter and mind are abstractions or conceptualizations. These conceptualizations are of 17th-century physics, and have become inadequate in modern science. "Matter" has dematerialized in modern physics—that is, there are ultimately not tiny hard corpuscles according to classical physics but what remains, are minute agglomerations of energy in space separated by astronomical distances; speaking more precisely, an undefined entity or unknown X, certain properties of which are expressed by very abstract conservation laws of modern physics. Mind, on the other hand, is not Descartes' thinking or conscious substance any more. According to the testimony of psychology, conscious phenomena are, as it were, crests of waves of processes in the unconscious, waves which, for unknown reasons, we experience. This is another X or reality which in its manifestations is researchable and describable by psychology.

The third problem is the neuro-psychological. There are relations between the brain as a physical object, and mental processes. Why certain processes in neurons and in the brain are connected with consciousness or awareness, while the overwhelming multitude of neural events is not, we have no idea. It is obvious, however, that we cannot correlate "physical and chemical processes" in the conventional sense with mental processes. Chemical reactions in the retina or brain, electric currents in nerves, chemical transmission of hormone-like substances at the synapses—these and similar things have not the faintest resemblance or comparability with seeing red color, feeling sad, deciding to make a trip and the like.

However, when we extend the vision of conventional science, we discover something interesting. General system concepts such as organization, goal-directedness, differentiation, development and the like did not exist in conventional science; you will look in vain for such terms in the textbooks of physics and chemistry. However, the biologist, the psychologist and sociologist cannot do without them. To the biologist, an organism is not a heap of physical and chemical processes but a functional organization; and something similar applies to the psychologist's and sociologist's considerations. This, of course, was the reason why an expansion of scientific concepts and models was sought in systems theory. And we are able to say that such models or concepts are, and increasingly become, available in systems theory. Hence we can speak of goal-seeking, self-organizing, etc., systems in a scientific way—that is, of systems and models concerning aspects beyond the mechanistic scheme, and comparable to those found in "mental" experience. These also are characteristic of that mysterious unconscious, a part of which, the crest of the wave, is experienced in consciousness. There may, therefore, be a formal correspondence or isomorphism between the two realms of phenomena called, for short, brain and mind. Not indeed a correspondence of individual physical and chemical reactions in the brain with mental phenomena, or a reduction of mental phenomena to physical and chemical ones; but rather an isomorphism of structure in much more general and abstract terms, which are being stated in systems theory. Eventually, there might be unitary models covering both fields.

Arieti (1968) asked in a recent paper: "I cannot see how these theories" (meaning systems theory in the sense discussed) "can explain the phenomenon of subjective or private experience." I (i.e. the present author) cannot see this either, but this is precisely the limitation of physical and indeed of any scientific theory. If we parallel Arieti's statement with respect to "objective" or "public experience," we must similarly say: "I cannot see how physics can explain the phenomena of objective or public experience." Indeed, that, how, and why elementary particles or, if you like, high-energy parcels, widely diffused in space, make for the solid table standing before our noses is completely unexplainable by physics. The answer is simply that science, be it conventional "physics and chemistry" or the expansion called "systems theory," never gives more than models for (to an extent) handling and controlling reality, in the way of appropriate conceptual constructs. But what "reality" ultimately is behind the phenomena of both subjective and objective experience remains beyond the limitations and even the interests of science. However, it may well be that we have other access to this reality in direct experience and its sublimation in art, music, mystical knowledge.

CONCLUSION

When starting the present considerations, I said that the modern development of systems theory essentially tends toward an expanion of scientific theory and world view. I also said that these theoretical developments can well be used in the service of further mechanization of man, in' making him a wheel in the megamachine, in frustrating his individuality. In contrast to this dismal view, I hope that, with the progress of our considerations, it has become apparent that this approach (systems theory) is a profoundly humanistic one. To summarize in the shortest possible way: The mechanistic universe appeared as a world of chaos, of chance play of atoms, of blind forces of nature, of evolution by way of random mutations and utilitarian selection. Now we begin to see, or try to see, the world as a great organization, lawfully ascending from the ultimate particles of physics to living organisms and eventually to man and his supra-individual socio-symbolic systems; at the same time taking into account the specifics of each level: physical systems, organisms with their marvellous order of parts and processes, man with his unique universe of culture. Furthermore, the systems view is not scientism but what I like to call a perspective philosophy. This is to say that science is one perspective of reality, one way to retrace reality in certain of its formal aspects; but there are other approaches too, in art, music, religion and so forth. Put differently, the systems approach can give some answer to the question of meaning, which is nothing else than connection within a whole or system.

In our society and civilization, we have carried a scientistic attitude to the extreme and landed in a mechanistic-behavioristic-commercialistic world which bears little resemblance to the utopia for which science, rationalism, and belief in progress had hoped. Instead—it all seems so meaningless. There is, in Frankl's worlds, an existential vacuum experienced by the individual, with concomitant mental disease; not to mention again parallel phenomena in society, politics and elsewhere.

This basic trouble or sickness of our society appears to be at two levels. One seems to be that we stand at the end of a civilization, that present man and society appear to be post-historic, to use a fashionable catchword. That is, the majestic stream of Western culture, from medieval cathedrals to all the achievements of art, poetry, music, science and philosophy that have graced the past, appears exhausted and a new and strange civilization emerging (if we do not blow up the planet before)—a mass civilization of technological and global nature.

Beside this predicament of our time, there is, secondly, the general human predicament. It is the dualism of man in a natural and a symbolic (or cultural) world. As I once expressed it, man's forebrain has developed splendidly, and this made possible the evolution from stone axes to atom bombs, from fetishism to physics. The brainstem of man, however, seat of emotions, instincts, animal drives, did not evolve but remained pretty much the same since the dawn of man and his ape-like ancestors. The fact was emphasized by MacLean in his studies of the visceral brain, and brilliantly expounded by Arthur Koestler (1968) in his doctrine of the "three brains" of man. Here is the reason that we have an almost superhuman intellect which created atomic physics and bombs, combined with the subhuman instincts of a savage or angry ape.

As I attempted to show, the new science attempts to overcome the limitations of the mechanistic view, and in the very process, to reintroduce the human or humanistic element which was lost. It tries to give new answers to old questions and to control mistakes we obviously made in our scientistic world view and civilization. Whether in the turmoil of our time this may provide a respite, I do not know. We can only say that we have tried.

REFERENCES

1. ARDREY, R., *The Territorial Imperative,* New York, Dell Publishing Co., 1968.
2. ARIETI, S., "Schizophrenia." In S. Arieti, *Handbook of American Psychiatry,* Vol. I, New York: Basic Books, 1959.
3. ARIETI, S., Contributions to Cognition from Psychoanalytic Theory. In Masserman, G. (Ed.) *Science and Psychoanalysis* (Vol. 8). New York: Grune and Stratton, 1965.
4. BENEDICT, R., Patterns of Culture. (1934). New York: Mentor Books, 1946.
5. BUCKLEY, W., *Modern Systems Research for the Behavioral Scientist.* Chicago, Ill.: Aldine, 1967.
6. ELLIS, H. F., "The Naked Ape Crisis." The New Yorker, 1968.
7. FRANKL, V., *The Will to Meaning: Foundations and Applications of Logotherapy.* New York: World Publishing Co., 1969.
8. GIBSON, J. J., *The Senses Considered as Perceptual Systems.* Boston: Houghton, Mifflin, 1966.
9. GRAY, W., DUHL, F., and RIZZO, N., *General Systems Theory and Psychiatry.* Boston: Little, Brown and Co., 1969.
10. GRINKER, R. R. (Ed.), *Toward a Unified Theory of Human Behavior* (2nd ed.). New York: Basic Books, 1967.
11. KOESTLER, A., *The Act of Creation.* London: Hutchinson, 1964.
12. KOESTLER, A., *The Ghost in the Machine.* London, Hutchinson, 1968.
13. KUHN, T. S. *The Structure of Scientific Revolutions.* Chicago: University of Chicago Press, 1962.
14. LORENZ, K., *On Aggression.* New York: Harcourt, Brace and World, 1963.
15. MEIR, A., "General System Theory, Developments and Perspectives for Medicine and Psychiatry." *Arch. Gen. Psychiat.* 21, 302-310, 1969.
16. MENNINGER, K., MAYMAN, M., and PRUYSER, P. *The Vital Balance.* New York: The Viking Press, 1963.
17. MORRIS, D., *The Naked Ape.* New York: McGraw Hill, 1967.
18. MORRIS, D., *The Human Zoo.* New York: McGraw Hill, 1969.
19. MUMFORD, L. *The Myth of the Machine.* New York: Harcourt, Brace and World, 1967.
20. OPLER, M., *Culture, Psychology and Human Values.* Springfield, Ill.: Thomas, 1956.
21. ROYCE, J. R., *The Encapsulated Man.* New York: Van Nostrand, 1964.
22. TIGER, L., *Men in Groups.* New York: Random House, 1967.
23. VON BERTALANFFY, L., *General System Theory. Foundations, Development, Applications.* New York: Braziller, 1968.
24. VON BERTALANFFY, L., *Robots, Men and Minds.* New York: Braziller, 1967.
25. VON BERTALANFFY, L., Some Considerations on the Problem of Mental Illness. In L. Appleby, J. Scher, and J. Cummings (Eds.) *Chronic Schizophrenia.* Glencoe (Ill.): The Free Press, 1960.
26. VON BERTALANFFY, L., The Mind-Body Problem: A New View, *Psychosomatic Medicine* 24: 29-45, 1964.
27. VON BERTALANFFY, L., Mind and Body Re-Examined. *Journal of Humanistic Psychology* 6: 113-138, 1966.

5

The Inner World of Man: Biochemical Substrates of Affect and Memory

SEYMOUR S. KETY, M.D.

Professor of Psychiatry, Harvard Medical School
Director of Psychiatric Research Laboratories,
Massachusetts General Hospital

The important progress in molecular biology which has revolutionized biology and genetics has not yet made its major contribution to the nervous system and behavior. In the biology of behavior we have seen a number of important achievements in recent years. There have been significant advances in the physiological processes and anatomical substrates involved in the processing of sensory information. We have seen electronic averaging techniques applied to the electroencephalogram making it possible to display with great fidelity the curve of electrical events associated in the human cortex with specific sensory inputs and mental states. Perhaps it is in the fields of neurochemistry and neuropharmacology that there has been recent progress of most immediate promise to psychiatry, permitting at least the formulation of concepts regarding mood and memory. Because these two qualities of the human brain are crucially important to human values and experience, they seem most appropriate as the focus of my discussion. I should like to examine some of the information we have and the speculations we can derive regarding the mental states of mood, affect, and emotion.

Present knowledge rests firmly upon the work of Walter Cannon and Philip Bard, in two different aspects of the field, and represents an interesting conjunction between them. Cannon recognized the role of the peripheral sympathetics and the hormones associated with them—epinephrine and norepinephrine, in mediating the somatic adjustments necessary and appropriate for emotional states. The fight or flight responses of Cannon can be expanded to include the appetitive responses for food or mating and a variety of adaptations necessary for the survival of the individual or of the race. Philip Bard pioneered in the regions within the brain necessary for the mediation and the sustenance of these states i.e. the hypothalamus, amygdala, and other regions of the rhinencephalon—regions which were later to be organized into a system—the limbic system or the visceral brain. It probably did not occur to either of these great scientists that one of the substances which Cannon was examining and which he believed to be involved in the peripheral manifestations of affective state was also being secreted within the brain by particular neurons, richly distributed within the system which Bard was studying, and, quite possibly, mediating its effects. There are tides of evidence, as difficult to deny as more specifically and rigorously to define, that certain amines of the brain may be biochemical substrates of emotion, and that protein synthesis within the brain may be crucially involved in the laying down of memory. I should like to indicate some of the evidence for the relationship of these biochemical substrates to their suggested behavioral functions and then attempt a highly speculative but hopefully heuristic hypothesis of how these neurochemical processes may be linked to explain the well-known linkage of affect and memory in the process of learning.

Although there is much to be learned regarding the mechanisms of release and action of neurotransmitters at peripheral synapses, a transmitter function appears well established for norepinephrine, as is its peripheral involvement along with epinephrine in emotional expression (1). In the brain, however, no biogenic amine has been conclusively shown to be a transmitter, nor even to be specifically associated with a particular behavioral or affective state. The evidence is indirect and inferential but sufficiently extensive and consistent, nevertheless, to permit the formulation of hypotheses that central as well as peripheral actions of biogenic amines mediate arousal and emotion.

By means of the characteristic fluorescence of their condensation products after reaction with formalin vapor, serotonin and catecholamines have been demonstrated throughout the brain and spinal cord, concentrated in the presynaptic varicosities along the terminal axons of particular neurons (2). Their cell-bodies themselves appear to be clustered in the brain-stem, the serotonin-containing neurons in the midline raphé nuclei and those containing catecholamines more laterally disposed with a high density in the locus ceruleus. Axons from those amine-containing neurons pass downward into the spinal cord and upward by way of the medial forebrain bundle to innervate most of the brain. There are especially high densities of their terminals in the various nuclei of the hypothalamus but the entire cerebral cortex and even the cerebellar cortex contain many very fine fibers with the characteristic serotonin or catecholamine fluorescence which is intensified after treatment with monoamine ovidase inhibitors and diminishes following reserpine or medial forebrain bundle lesions. Sufficient attention has been given to norepinephrine in the brain and its possible relationship to mood to permit using that amine as an example of the group without suggesting that it has a predominant or exclusive role.

The early studies relied upon the total content of norepinephrine in the brain or its concentration in particular regions. Thus, Barchas and Freedman (3) showed a decrease in this amine in the brain along with an increase in serotonin in rats forced to swim to exhaustion. Maynert and Levi (4) found a 40% decrease in norepinephrine in the brainstem after thirty minutes of foot shocks. Reis and Gunne (5) induced rage in cats by stimulating the amygdala and demonstrated a highly significant decrease in the norepinephrine levels of the telencephalon. More recent studies have confirmed the relationship between induced rage and norepinephrine levels in the brain and have adduced further evidence for the crucial involvement of this amine in that form of behavior by augmenting and inhibiting the manifestations of rage by drugs which respectively potentiate and block the pharmacologic actions of norepinephrine (6).

Closer to the dynamic relationships involved in synthesis and release is the examination of the turnover of norepinephrine in the brain. If synthesis is coupled to release in the central nervous system as it appears to be in the periphery, simple levels of the endogenous amine would reflect only disparities between the two processes and not the magnitude of either. On the other hand, the disappearance of labelled amine from a pool into which it had been introduced would be affected by alterations in its rate of release, even though these were completely compensated by corresponding changes in synthesis. Although norepinephrine does not cross the blood:brain barrier the tritium-labelled amine is rapidly distributed to various parts of the brain after intraventricular or intracisternal injection and concentrated at presynaptic endings, largely of norepinephrine-containing neurons (7). The disappearance of the labelled amine from the brain does not follow a mono-exponential curve, suggesting the presence of two or more compartments with different rates of turnover. Its initial slope, however, should approximate the average turnover rate and the decrements over standard periods of time have been used for qualitative comparison of turnover rates between experimental and control groups of animals. An alternative method of examining turnover rate is afforded by following the curve of disappearance of the endogenous amine after blocking its synthesis by means of α-methyltyrosine (8). Although this technique does not require the use of exogenous material and obviates questions regarding the specificity of the material the turnover of which is being examined, it requires the assumption that turnover rate is independent of endogenous levels and would not be expected to reflect changes in rate of turnover brought about by changes in synthesis, since the latter process is blocked.

In addition to yielding valuable information on the effects of drugs on norepinephrine metabolism, rate of turnover has also been examined in some behavioral states where it has been found to be more sensitive and informative than study of endogenous levels alone. In foot shock of milder form than that used previously, it was possible to demonstrate a significant increase in turnover throughout the brain and spinal cord with no systematic change in endogenous levels of the amine (9). This suggested an augmented synthesis coupled with release which has been demonstrated more directly in the periphery. Repeated exposure to such stress over a period of three days was associated with a significant elevation of endogenous levels of the amine, further supporting the hypothesis that synthesis was stimulated, and compatible with an induction of the rate-limiting enzyme.

The turnover of norepinephrine was found to be substantially increased after one week of a regimen of twice daily electroconvulsive shocks and 24 hours after the last shock, at a time when the behavior of the animals was quite normal. This, coupled with a significant elevation in endogenous norepinephrine, implied a persistent increase in synthesis of the amine (10). An increase in tyrosine hydroxylase levels in the brain was demonstrated in animals 24 hours after the same regimen of electroconvulsive shocks (11).

The drugs effective in relieving clinical depression (amphetamine, monoamine oxidase inhibitors, imipramine) all affect norepinephrine turnover or metabolism in the brain in ways which would be expected to increase the activity of that amine in central synapses, while drugs causing depression have an opposite effect (12). The finding that electroconvulsive shock, which is probably the most effective treatment for depression, could also increase the availability of norepinephrine at synapses in the brain in this instance by increasing its synthesis, is also compatible with the possibility that a deficiency of that amine may exist in the brain in some states of depression.

Pharmacological tools in conjunction with a form of appetitive behavior have been used to adduce evidence that norepinephrine may be involved in the "reward" system in the brain. Stein has examined the effects of various drugs on the self-stimulating behavior in rats described by Olds and Milner and has found that imipramine or amphetamine will significantly increase such activity, while reserpine will suppress it (13). The effects of amphetamine are greatly diminished following reserpine or α-methyltyrosine. The most parsimonious explanation of all these observations is that this form of appetitive behavior requires the intervention of one of the catecholamines. The conditional avoidance response is another form of behavior which can be blocked by drugs which deplete catecholamine stores in the brain or by lesions in the postero-lateral hypothalamic mid-brain junction or medial forebrain bundle which result in a loss of serotonin and norepinephrine from much of the telencephalon. The effects of catecholamine depleting drugs are rather specific since they can be demonstrated while escape behavior is unaffected. Depletion of serotonin alone is apparently insufficient to affect conditioned avoidance.

Correlations of turnover rates of biogenic amines with behavioral states or the ability of drugs which affect amines in the brain to alter behavior offer evidence which is compatible with hypotheses that one or another amine is involved in a particular form of behavior. Such evidence hardly constitutes proof, however, since alternative explanations of the various findings must usually be entertained. Better evidence would be the demonstration of the release of a particular putative transmitter in the brain in constant association with a specific type of behavior as had been achieved for acetylcholine, norepinephrine and gamma-aminobutyric acid at particular peripheral synapses. Brain slices have been shown to release norepinephrine or other amine when stimulated with electrical current or potassium ion, or when exposed to low concentrations of certain drugs. Lithium ion administered *in vivo* or added *in vitro* appears to block the stimulated release of norepinephrine or serotonin from brain slices, suggesting that lithium ion, rather specifically effective in treating mania, may act by inhibiting the release of biogenic amines.

Although a release of norepinephrine from the brain *in vivo* has been reported in association with appetitive stimulation the specificity of the release was not established; in other experiments neuronal activation has been found to release not only norepinephrine but also urea and inulin. On the other hand, d-amphetamine has been found to release norepinephrine and its methylated metabolite, but not inulin, from the brain.

The ability of acetylcholine or norepinephrine applied locally on "receptor" regions of a post-synaptic structure to elicit a response that closely mimics the effects of neurostimulation, functionally, electrically and pharmacologically, is good evidence that these substances are neurotransmitters at certain peripheral synapses. For that reason the effects of putative transmitters applied locally in the brain have been of considerable interest. When norepinephrine is injected into the ventricles, or intravenously in animals with a poorly developed blood: brain barrier, the effect produced is not arousal, but in practically every instance, some form of somnolence (14). The microinjection of this amine in the region of individual cells while their electrical activity is being recorded usually produces an inhibition of spontaneous activity. These observations do not necessarily argue against an important involvement of norepinephrine in arousal, since neither the dose nor the site of application is controlled in the first type of experiment, while an inhibition of random and spontaneous activity throughout the brain may constitute a characteristic feature of arousal with a facilitation of only small, sharply focused and specifically activated regions, which may have gone undetected in the recording of unit activity.

On the other hand, the elicitation of particular forms of behavior following more specific administration of the amine would suggest its involvement in similar types of natural activity. A number of such observations have been reported. Wise and Stein (15) suppressed self-stimulation (through electrodes in the medial forebrain bundle of rats) by the administration of diethyldithiocarbamate or disulfiram which blocks dopamine β-hydroxylase and depletes the brain of norepinephrine but not of dopamine. In such animals, the appetitive behavior could be restored by intraventricular injection of 1-norepinephrine (5 μg) but not by the dextro-isomer, or by dopamine or serotonin.

Slangen and Miller (16) have carried out a series of well-designed experiments which strongly suggest the involvement of norepinephrine in a type of feeding behavior. By implanting fine cannulae into the perifornical region at the posterior portion of the anterior hypothalamus, they were able to test the effects of various substances on a region where electrical stimulation is known to induce eating in a previously satiated rat. Small doses of 1-norepinephrine (20 μg moles) were found promptly to elicit the same type of behavior while serotonin had no effect. Dopamine induced no immediate change in behavior but a delayed and weak eating response, compatible with its conversion to norepinephrine. This region responded to other pharmacological agents as do norepinephrine (or alpha) receptors in the periphery. Phentolamine, which blocks alpha receptors, antagonized the norepinephrine response, while a beta receptor stimulant (isoproterenol) or antagonist (propranolol) had no effects *per se* or on the norepinephrine response. The norepinephrine-induced behavior was potentiated eight-fold by previous treatment of the animal with desipramine. An effect was also obtained from tetrabenazine, which releases norepinephrine and other amines from storage depots, provided monoamine oxidase had previously been blocked by nialimide. It is difficult to avoid the interpretation that this behavior is mediated by the release of norepinephrine acting on specific adrenergic receptors in this region.

Even the intraventricular administration of norepinephrine need not always lead to generalized sedation. Segal and Mandell (17) have observed activation and improved performance on a continuous avoidance task in animals receiving a constant infusion of low concentrations of norepinephrine; the activated behavior gave way to sedation with higher concentration.

The correlations such as those I have reviewed which suggest some role for the norepinephrine-containing neurons of the brain in affective behavior by no means deny the operation of other amines such as serotonin and dopamine in these or other states. In fact, there are some reports which show a better correlation between dopamine and arousal, activity and aggression than that which is found for norepinephrine. It is in fact extremely unlikely that a particular affective state is associated with only one of these amines or can possibly be equated even with an interaction between them. Whereas the function of some organs such as the liver or skeletal muscle may be thought of as a simple sum of the functions of its component cells which are small replicas of the whole, the brain is unique, for its neurons, even those with similar morphology and chemistry, differ markedly from each other. The function of a neuron is very largely determined by where it is, with what neurons it is connected, and what has been its past history. It is because chemical processes act not directly on the brain but on the highly specific and complex networks of units which comprise it, that behavior can never be reduced to neurochemistry.

The apperceptive mass of an individual can be thought of as representing some of those interrelationships incorporating the present situation and the past experience. Neurochemical and pharmacological studies of affect must take into consideration the interactions between chemistry and the apperceptive mass. There is always evidence that the effects of circulating epinephrine depend upon such cognitive factors. Schachter (18) has found that the same dose of epinephrine may produce anxiety, hostility, or hilarity, depending upon the individual and the environmental cues at his disposal. Similarly, I would think that neurohumoral and neurochemical processes may determine the volume and the key in the rendition of human behavior while the melody is largely provided by these idiosyncratic apperceptive factors.

I should like to offer some speculative hypotheses of how neurochemical factors and specifically the biogenic amines may operate in the acquisition and consolidation of the apperceptive mass. Let us consider first what are the adaptive purposes which are served by the affective response. We can point out a number that are classical. The emotional state activates muscular, endocrine, and autonomic systems to appropriate preparatory and consummatory experiences. The affects of anger or rage are associated with hypothalamic and autonomic stimulation which releases epinephrine and norepinephrine in the circulation and mobilizes blood sugar, increases the blood supply to muscles and the heart, and makes the animal ready for fight or flight. Other affective states do many other things beside preparation for fight and flight; they are involved in the autonomic, endocrine, and muscular responses necessary for exploring, foraging, eating, courting, mating—in fact all of the adaptive responses crucial to survival of the individual or the species. But in addition, emotional states play an essential role in the process of learning. Psychologists have known for some time that the intensity of affect associated with an experience determines to a large extent its acquisition and retention. I should like to develop a hypothesis regarding the biological substrates of that association and the adaptive purposes they serve.

From the teleological point of view it is not enough for an animal to remember all of its past experience. The adaptive advantage made possible by behavior which is learned by individual experience, over that which is wired-in genetically is that learned behavior is more finely tuned to the anticipated vicissitudes of the individual's experience, while that which is genetically endowed can only be an abstract of millions of years of the experience of the species. If learning is to have survival value it must rule out experiences which are irrelevant to that goal, reinforce those which are, and endow them with appropriate avoidance or appetitive qualities which may guide future behavior.

It is probable that we are endowed genetically with a system for evaluating current experience in terms of its survival value. Such a system would operate on the basis of a few relatively simple generalizations: inputs which are familiar and have not in the past been associated with deleterious effects are to be ignored. On the other hand, a new input, such as a novel experience, the outcome of which cannot be predicted, or one which in the past has been found to be followed by significant effects should be attended. Secondly, such a system should be able to discriminate between outcomes which are good and outcomes which are bad in terms of the general experience of the species. Thus, in its simplest form it would label as good and with appetitive overtones those experiences which are followed by the injestion of food and drink, copulation and other outcomes with a positive survival value. It would label as bad and to be avoided those outcomes which cause destruction of tissue, disturbance of homeostasis, and a host of outcomes deleterious to survival. It would want to assure that those experiences loaded with salutary or noxious components are remembered and in association with the components.

I should like to think that the diffuse system of mono-amine-containing neurons with their cell bodies in the brain stem and their axons ramifying throughout the limbic system and neocortex are, in fact, such a built-in system for discriminating between and facilitating the memory of new experiences significant to survival. Their distribution to the classical sensory-motor systems of the brain and the ability of local microinjection of monoamines to inhibit and occasionally to stimulate cortical neurons would be compatible with their playing a modulating role on the classical systems, mediating arousal and attention.

But more important, I can imagine ways in which the release of biogenic amines at sensory-motor and association synapses could affect learning. Much evidence indicates that experience is first held in a very temporary storage, probably electrical in nature, and only after an elapsed time, between a few minutes and an hour, is the temporary storage converted to a more permanent form of consolidation. It is the latter phase of memory which is blocked by inhibitors of protein synthesis in the brain. In fact, the one conclusion which one can draw from the work of many of the best contributors to the field of the biochemical substrate of memory, is that protein synthesis is essential to the consolidation of memory.

The two phases of the storage process may also have an important adaptive function. The first holds the information tentatively, awaiting an outcome and the judgment of the evaluative system of whether to discard or to retain and what value to associate in the retaining. By regulating protein synthesis at particular synapses the affective state generated by the interaction of outcome on the wired-in judgment system could determine the intensity and the affective coloration of the memory, and it could do so by releasing at the synapses a biogenic amine which facilitated protein synthesis and the consideration of memory.

There are some precedents for suggesting that small molecules like amines may regulate protein synthesis in the brain. In development, evidence suggests that various chemical factors direct protein synthesis to achieve the normal growth. The importance of thyroxin in the dendritic proliferation which accompanies maturation of the cerebral cortex is well established and the work of Sokoloff (19) which demonstrated a stimulant effect of that hormone on protein synthesis in the immature brain elucidates the cytological and behavioral effects of thyroxin there. There is now much evidence which suggests that norepinephrine in the periphery and in the brain as well acts by stimulating the production of cyclic AMP after its release and equally compelling evidence that this important, high-energy substance is involved in the initiation of protein synthesis in these tissues.

To elaborate further this one hypothesis, let us examine some more of the requirements of our postulated system for labelling and storing new experiences in terms of their significance to survival. If the organism is to take full advantage of these mechanisms and to profit maximally from idiosyncratic experience, it should not be partial to any sensory modality but receptive to all. Having screened out the trivial and familiar by the processes of habituation and attention, all the novel concomitants of the situation should be eligible for reinforcement and retention when the evaluators indicate a more than passing significance to the outcome. This would undoubtedly involve the temporary reinforcement of numerous irrelevant connections which, in common with those that happen to be relevant, would have an inherent tendency to decay. The repetitive trials which are required for most learning, however, should effectively reinforce the constantly recurring associations while permitting the cancellation of the random and adventitious ones, much as the modern computers of average transients operate. Ideally then, the input which reinforces on the basis of outcome should not be applied in some predesigned manner to selected circuits but indiscriminately to all or at least to all which were novel and which familiarity had not suppressed.

A number of observations have recently been made which lend some credence to such a hypothesis and suggest one or more sites where such amine-stimulated consolidation could occur. Scheibel and Scheibel (20) have described multibranched axons of cells in the brain stem which make synapses with thousands of neurons up and down the neuraxis. They have also described in greater detail the architectonics of the 'unspecific afferents' to the cerebral cortex with evidence that these long-climbing axons of cells in the thalamus and possibly in lower nuclei weave about the apical dendrites of pyramidal cells with an extremely loose axodendritic association in contrast to the vast number of well-defined synapses established by the terminals of the 'specific afferents.' In 1968, Fuxe, Hamberger and Hökfelt (21) described the terminations of the norepinephrine-containing axons in the cortex, pointing out the similarities in their distribution to that of the unspecific afferents of Scheibel and Scheibel.

If the unspecific afferents are indeed "adrenergic" or "aminergic" terminals invading the millions of sensory-sensory and sensory-motor synapses of the cortex, they would provide a remarkably effective mechanism whereby amines released in arousal could affect a crucial population of synapses throughout the brain. The hippocampal and cerebellar cortex are also characterized by "climbing fibers" some of which carry norepinephrine, and Bloom has come close to establishing a transmitter role for that amine between the terminals of certain climbing fibers and Purkinje cells. There is even some evidence that axons from the same adrenergic neuron in the brain stem may be distributed to cerebral, hippocampal and cerebellar cortex as well as to hypothalamus and many other areas of the brain and spinal cord. Marr has proposed a novel theory of the cerebellar cortex which implies a "learning" of patterns of motor activity by that structure. It is not impossible that by similar and simultaneous processes the state of arousal may serve concurrently to reinforce and consolidate the significant sensory, affective and motor networks necessary in the learning of a new adaptive response.

Just as the peripheral expressions of arousal and effect are mediated by both neurogenic and endocrine processes, it is possible that the central effects employ humoral as well as neural modes. There is a great tendency for these apical dendrites and their afferents, in a remarkably similar fashion in the cerebrum, hippocampus and cerebellum, to seek the cortical surface; indeed, the cortical convolutions which increase that surface several fold must have some adaptive function. Engineering necessity and developmental history have been invoked to explain this phenomenon, but it is also possible that these structures by virtue of being in close proximity to the cerebrospinal fluid serve another important adaptive function. The constant flow of this medium from the ventricles over the whole cortical surface on its way to the arachnoid villi offers a means of superfusing the cortex with substances derived from the blood stream at the choroid plexus or intracerebrally secreted by various stations along its path. It is noteworthy that ^{3}H-norepinephrine injected into one ventricle or into the cisterna magna rapidly penetrates the superficial layers of the brain; since the amines do not easily pass the blood:brain barrier and would not readily be removed by the capillaries, such a mechanism would further assure the widespread distribution of any which may be released from endings near the cortical surface. Acetylcholine and prostalglandins, which have been shown to be released there by neuronal activity, as well as also GABA, cyclic-AMP and a host of other substances, could be broadcast by this process.

Releasing factors of the hypothalamus, trophic hormones of the pituitary and the steroid hormones of the adrenal cortex, some of which are regularly secreted in states of arousal and stress, could thus have additional access to this rich population of synapses. Many of these substances have, in one system or another, displayed a capacity to stimulate the synthesis of RNA or of protein. The steroid hormones and ACTH clearly affect conditioning and, in addition to their well-established activities, induce enzymes in other tissues; one of them has recently been found to restore tryptophan hydroxylase activity in the midbrain of the adrenalectomized rat. It is tempting to speculate upon the possible trophic actions of such stress-related hormones or cortical synapses.

A substantial number of recent observations would have been predicted by this hypothesis which may also help to account for certain difficulties or inconsistencies. RNA and protein synthesis have both been found to be stimulated at sites of increased neuronal activity (22), but inconsistently so, perhaps because the crucial contingent factor of arousal has not been held constant. Conversely, Roberts and Flexner (23) have pointed out that the increased protein synthesis demonstrated by some experiments during learning is considerably greater than would be required by the newly-established neuronal patterns, unless a generalized facilitation of synthesis of new protein occurred which then decayed except for that in the repeatedly reinforced patterns.

The hypothesis would predict that drugs which release or enhance norepinephrine in the brain or exert its neuronal effects would favor consolidation and facilitate memory. Amphetamine and caffeine appear capable of producing such effects, and recently a more specific ability of amphetamine or foot-shock to counteract the suppression of consolidation brought about by cyclohexamide has been reported (24).

Conversely, lesions or drugs which deplete or block norepinephrine in the brain should retard consolidation and prevent acquisition. Although there are many reports on the ability of such drugs (reserpine, α-methyl tyrosine) to block the established conditioned-avoidance response, there is no information on their effects during acquisition. Recently, however, W. B. Essman (personal communication) has found a significant impairment in acquisition, following α-methyl tyrosine, which was most intense when the brain levels of norepinephrine were lowest. Lesions of the medial forebrain bundle which would be expected to deplete the telencephalon of norepinephrine and serotonin, appeared in one study to depress acquisition (25).

The suggestion that the release of norepinephrine may favor consolidation of learning by stimulating protein synthesis is made more tenable by recently acquired information on the possible action of cyclic AMP in the brain. This substance, present in surprisingly high concentration in the central nervous system as is adenyl cyclase, the enzyme which brings about its synthesis, is crucially involved in enzyme induction and protein synthesis in a wide variety of bacterial and mammalian cells and appears to induce protein synthesis in brain mitochondria. Evidence is accumulating that cyclic AMP may mediate the effects of norepinephrine on central neurons as it is believed to do for the actions of catecholamines and other hormones on liver, muscle and other peripheral tissues (26).

The early hypotheses which assigned an important role to central norepinephrine and other biogenic amines in mediating emotional states have stimulated considerable research. It is hoped that these speculations regarding their possible function in the biochemical processes which underlie memory and learning may be of some heuristic value.

I should like to emphasize that my concern in this presentation has been very largely with the machinery of behavior —the mechanisms by which these complex responses are brought about. As must be apparent, our knowledge of these biological mechanisms is fragmentary and pieced together by highly speculative bridges. Complicated as the machinery is, however, it is only a small part of the basis of human behavior, which though mediated by biological mechanisms is to a considerable extent determined by the information which the machinery has processed and stored over a lifetime. The biologist is most pretentious who assumes that he can arrive at an understanding of this information, stored as it is in the complex interaction of ten billion neurons, simply through the use of biological techniques (27). The simple symbol CAT, whether it be the printed word or the pattern of neuronal activity which it induces in the visual cortex, cannot by all the physico-chemical techniques in the world be reduced to a simpler form which will somehow explain its meaning. The particular geometrical arrangement of graphite particles has its meaning only by reference to human experience and can be explained only in terms of information and communication processes. There will someday be a biochemistry of memory but hardly ever one of memories. Since so much of human behavior depends upon the apperceptive mass of the individual and the experiential information which it incorporates, it is only by an appropriate collaboration between biology and the sciences which deal with information and experience that an understanding of human behavior will be approached.

REFERENCES

1. KETY, S. S. Catecholamines in neuropsychiatric states. *Pharmacol. Rev.* 18: 787-798, 1966.

2. HILLARP, N. A., FUXE, K., and DAHLSTROM, A. Demonstration and mapping of the central neurons containing dopamine, noradrenaline, and 5-hydroxytryptamine and their reactions to psychopharmaca. *Pharmacol. Rev.* 18: 727-741, 1966.

3. BARCHAS, J. D. and FREEDMAN, D. Response to physiological stress. *Biochem. Pharmacol.* 12: 1232-1235, 1963.

4. MAYNERT, E. W. and LEVI, R. Stress induced released of brain norepinephrine and its inhibition by drugs. *J. Pharmacol. Exp. Ther.* 143: 90-95, 1964.

5. REIS, D. J. and GUNNE, L. M. Brain catecholamines: reaction to the defense reaction evoked by amygdaloid stimulation in cat. *Science* 149: 450-451, 1965.

6. REIS, D. J. and FUXE, K. Brain norepinephrine: evidence that neuronal release is essential for sham rage behavior following brainstem transection in cat. *Proc. Nat. Acad. Sci.* (USA) 64: 108-112, 1969.

7. GLOWINSKI, J. and AXELROD, J. Effects of drugs on the disposition of H3-norepinephrine in the rat brain. *Pharmacol. Rev.* 18: 775-785, 1966.

8. COSTA, E. and NEFF, N. H. Isotopic and nonisotopic measurements of catecholamine biosynthesis. In Biochemistry and Pharmacology of the Basal Ganglia, E. Costa, L. Cote, and M. D. Yahr, Eds., Raven Press, New York, 1966.

9. THIERRY, A. M., JAVOY, F., GLOWINSKI, J., and KETY, S. S. Effects of stress on the metabolism of norepinephrine, dopamine, and serotonin in the central nervous system of the rat. I. Modifications of norepinephrine turnover. *J. Pharmacol. Exp. Ther.* 163: 163, 1968.

10. KETY, S. S., JAVOY, F., THIERRY, A.-M., JULOU, L., and GLOWINSKI, J. A sustained effect of electroconvulsive shock on the turnover of norepinephrine in the central nervous system of the rat. *Proc. Nat. Acad. Sci.* (USA) 58: 1249-1254, 1967.

11. MUSACCHIO, J. M., JULOU, L., KETY, S. S. and GLOWINSKI, J. Increase in rat brain tyrosine hydroxylase activity produced by electroconvulsive shock. *Proc. Nat. Acad. Sci.* (USA) 63: 1117-1119, 1969.

12. KETY, S. S. The central physiological and pharmacological effects of the biogenic amines and their correlations with behavior. In: The Neurosciences, A Study Program, G. C. Quarton, T. Melnechuk, and F. O. Schmitt, Eds. Rockefeller University Press, New York, pp. 441-451, 1967.

13. STEIN, L. Self-stimulation of the brain and the central stimulant action of amphetamine. *Fed. Proc.* 23: 836-850, 1964.

14. MANDELL, A. J. and SPOONER, C. E. Psychochemical research studies in man. *Science* 162: 1442-1453, 1968.

15. WISE, C. D. and STEIN, L. Facilitation of brain self-stimulation by central administration of norepinephrine. *Science* 163: 299-301, 1969.
16. SLANGEN, J. L. and MILLER, N. E. Pharmacological tests for the function of hypothalamic norepinephrine in eating behavior. *Physiol. Behav.* 4: 543-552, 1969.
17. SEGAL, D. S. and MANDELL, A. J. The effects of chronic intraventricular infusion of norepinephrine in rats performing on a continuous avoidance task. *Proc. Nat. Acad. Sci.* (USA), (in press).
18. SCHACHTER, S. and SINGER, J. E. Cognitive, social and physiological determinants of emotional state. *Psychol. Rev.* 69: 379-399, 1962.
19. SOKOLOFF, L. The action of thyroid hormones and cerebral development. *Amer. J. Dis. Child.* 114: 498-506, 1967.
20. SCHEIBEL, M. E. and SCHEIBEL, A. B. Structural organization of non-specific thalamic nuclei and their projection toward cortex. *Brain Res.* 6: 60-94, 1967.
21. FUXE, K., HAMBERGER, B., and HOKFELT, T. Distribution of noradrenalin nerve terminals in cortical areas of the rat. *Brain Res.* 8: 125-131, 1968.
22. GLASSMAN, E. The biochemistry of learning: an evaluation of the rate of RNA and protein. *Ann. Rev. Biochem.* 38: 605-646, 1969.
23. ROBERTS, R. B. and FLEXNER, L. B. The biochemical basis of long-term memory. *Quart. Rev. Biophys.* 2: 135-173, 1969.
24. BARONDES, J. D. and FREEDMAN, D. Response to physiological stress. *Biochem. Pharmacol.* 12: 1232-1235, 1963.
25. SHEARD, M. H., APPEL, J. B. and FREEDMAN, D. X. The effect of central nervous system lesions on brain monoamines and behavior. *J. Psychiat. Res.* 5: 237-242, 1967.
26. SIGGINS, G. R., HOFFER, B. J., and BLOOM, F. E. Cyclic adenosine monophosphate: possible mediator for norepinephrine effects of cerebellar Purkinje cells. *Science* 165: 1018-1020, 1969.
27. KETY, S. S. A biologist examines the mind and behavior. Many disciplines contribute to understanding human behavior, each with peculiar virtues and limitations. *Science* 132: 1861-1870, 1960.

6

Man's Social and Cultural World

G. M. CARSTAIRS, M.D.
Professor of Psychiatry, University of Edinburgh

The common theme which recurs like a leit-motif in each of the Three Worlds of Man is *Adaptation*. This is shown most clearly in the long slow processes of biological evolution, which have endowed us with our extraordinarily complex equipment of organic systems, with the interior milieu of our bodily biochemistry, with our sense organs and with a repertoire of behavioral responses to environmental stimuli —all exquisitely adapted to the conditions of our life on this tiny planet.

The evolution of our physical make-up has been a slow, laborious process, spread over many millennia. It has resulted in the creation of a most peculiar species, whose success is attributable in large measure to our flexibility. Subgroups of homo-sapiens are able to feel at home in the Arctic, in the Kalahari desert, or on the high Andes! And even those of us who live in temperate climes have been able, in some degree, to come to terms with these extremes of climatic variation. As Dr. von Bertalanffy has observed, man himself has brought about great changes in his physical environment, in his diet and in the array of bacteria to which he formerly was exposed. Already we can control our indoor

climate, and before very long we may be able to do the
same out of doors, for whole countries and continents.

These two aspects of adaptation result in very gradual
changes in human physique and behavior, and in his sur-
roundings—although in the last few generations man's capacity to change—and all too often to despoil—his environment has become enormously accelerated. In contrast,
throughout recorded history the rate of change in our social
and cultural worlds has been conspicuously rapid.

It has been generally agreed for at least 20 years, among
students of human evolution, that the real growing point of
evolutionary change in our species now lies in the psycho-
social realm. Today, social and cultural changes are occurring
so rapidly that at times one has the feeling of watching a
film in which the action has been speeded up, in a manner
which is at first comical, but can become alarmingly chaotic.

Perhaps it would help to step back, for a moment or
two, in order to consider some other periods and peoples,
in which the rate of change was less frenetic.

Let me therefore turn back some two hundred and fifty
years, to April 23rd, 1719, to be precise—the date on which
a certain William Taylor, bookseller at the Ship in Paternos-
ter Row, London, entered in the Stationers' Register his
right to a whole share in a new book: "The Life and Strange
Surprizing Adventures of Robinson Crusoe of York, Mar-
iner: who lived eight and twenty years alone in an unin-
habited Island on the Coast of America, near the mouth of
the Great River Oroonoque. Having been cast on Shore by
Shipwreck, wherein all the Men perished but himself. With
an Account how he was at last strangely deliver'd by
Pyrates."

"Robinson Crusoe" won immediate and lasting acclaim.
It has re-appeared in over 300 editions in English, and in
almost as many different translations: it has been amended
and imitated many times, but still readers return to Daniel

Defoe's original story as they have done generation by generation.

Clearly, there is something very compelling about this fantasy, which rivets the attention of Russians, Turks and Chinese, no less than its readers in English. Why is this the case?

I suggest that its fascination lies in that it articulates for us our vague awareness of how helpless we should feel if we were suddenly cut off from our legacy of shared knowledge, and of cultural artifacts. We are forcibly reminded that our culture is as much part of us as is the shell which a snail laboriously makes and then carries forever on its back. Bereft of our culture, its know-how and its material products, we would all feel as naked and exposed as a snail without its shell.

This is why we empathize so strongly with Robinson Crusoe, who finds his loneliness so oppressive that he talks and prays aloud, long before he is joined by Man Friday; and this is why we are so involved in his struggle with the wilderness, in which he slowly, and painfully creates first a shelter, then a stockade, and eventually an area of cultivation.

It is interesting to reflect that this elemental drama has been re-enacted in imagination by successive generations of readers with a constantly changing cast. Although the essential antithesis remains the same—the confrontation of raw, elemental nature with man's drive to impose order and control (or as the French anthropologist Levi-Strauss has put it, the opposition of "le cru" and "le cuit")—the implicit paradigm of "civilized man" has changed, decade after decade.

One can be sure that Defoe's contemporaries scarcely doubted that they represented the acme of human achievement: and yet at that time they were still (although sporadically) burning witches in Britain; and fortunes were being made by British entrepreneurs who brought shiploads

of hapless African slaves to the colonies of North and South
America, even though one in five of their human merchan-
dise died before the voyage was over. The American colonists
still held only a precarious foothold on the Eastern seaboard
—while a French explorer had recently travelled from the
Illinois River down the Mississippi to the Gulf of Mexico,
claiming that whole territory for the King of France, after
whom he called it Louisiana.

Already, in the American settlements there was quietly
germinating a catalyst which was to quicken a spirit of
revolt against the long-established tradition-oriented societies of Western Europe. The great changes to be brought
about by their industrial revolution were still in the future;
but the germ of revolt against autocracy, not in favor of a
rival authority but inspired by belief in the rights of the
individual, was already beginning to grow.

Until this time, European explorers who penetrated into
South America, or India or China encountered societies at
least as complex, and as advanced in material accomplishments, as their own. In 1719—and still, 200 years later—the
great majority of the peoples of mankind lived a tribal or
at best a parochial existence in comparatively small communities, either relatively or in many cases absolutely cut
off from the wider world. For many years, anthropologists
focused their attention upon these separate small societies,
each of which was happily convinced that its values were
the only true values, that its customs represented the only
proper way to behave. Nor was this cultural solipsism confined to small, primitive societies; it was no less evident in
the determination with which Catholic Spain and Protestant
England sent out their missionaries to try to convince the
poor Indians—redskinned or brown—of the error of their
ways, to clothe them in European clothes and to instruct
them to build replicas of baroque cathedrals and tall-spired
churches in the most unlikely settings.

The functional school of anthropology, in which I was

tutored, regards each culture or society as an organization of means designed to achieve certain ends. These ends may be found in needs or impulses more or less biologically rooted, or, as Malinowski demonstrated in the economic cycle of the Kula exchange, in art forms, in religion and myth, they may be formulated in order to meet a people's social and psychological needs.

Functionalists were able to draw upon field observations of unprecedented richness of detail, following the example set by Malinowski in his four-year stay among the Trobiand Islanders. Functionalists drew attention to the infinite interconnectedness of all the institutions in each particular culture, each of which reflected a repertoire of perceptions, values and forms of interaction which was as consistent, as singular, and as arbitrary as the array of phonemes which their several languages had declared to be sounds which conveyed meaning.

Because the human being is so remarkably malleable, at least in his early years, the first systematic students of culture and personality particularly emphasized the importance of his early learning, and of all the socializing processes, the deliberate and the implicit indoctrination, which prepared him for his adult role. Some, following Benjamin Whorf, explored the ways in which a people's whole conceptual schemata could be shaped by the forms of their native speech. Others, influenced more or less directly by Freud, sought the origins of stereotyped adult behavior in the emotional interactions between children and their mothers, and other significant figures in their early upbringing.

It was unfortunate that early field research into cultural influences on personality development was carried out at a time when anthropologists had discarded, as largely irrelevant, the emphasis which earlier generations had placed upon genetic factors. We know only too well that genetic theories of personality and behavior can lead to oversimplifications, and can be perverted in the service of theories of

racial supremacy; but in the generation between the two
World Wars cultural anthropologists—and especially students of culture and personality—were so intent on stressing
the importance of social learning, mediated through child-
rearing practices and through socially defined roles and customs, that they tended to minimize, if not reject outright,
the role of inherited predisposition. Certainly, when compared with that of ants, bees or birds, human behavior
appears to consist overwhelmingly of learned, adaptive patterns rather than of fixed, stereotyped responses. However,
in recent years ethologists have made us re-think our old,
oversimplified concepts of instinct. Innate propensities of
behavior are no longer regarded simply as fixed stereotyped
channels of expression, as Instincts (re-ified with a capital
letter) which demand their gratification. Instead, instinctive
behavior is seen as the interaction of innate potentialities
of response and of action, which are quickened into life only
if certain categories of stimuli are offered at particular stages
in the animals' development, and which in turn are extin-
guished at the signal given by other, later stimuli.

It is easy to accept the evidence for such interactions
between innate propensities and timely external stimuli,
when ethologists spell out their meticulous studies of trigger
stimuli, releaser mechanisms and elements of behavioral response in the greylag goose, the stickleback, or the common
gull; but all this seemed far indeed from human experience.
It is only the more recent findings of ethologists who have
studied the higher primates in their natural habitat that
have brought the whole question of innate behavior patterns
back into human behavioral psychology—although Dr. von
Bertalanffy reminds us of the caution with which behavior
patterns in one species can be generalized by any other.

Here, I should like to acknowledge my own personal debt
to two outstanding mediating figures: to John Bowlby, who
has been the linkman between ethology and psychiatry, and
to another linkman, my anthropologist colleague Derek

Freedman. When we first met in Oxford 21 years ago he had already lived for two years in a Samoan village, studying social structure. Up to that point, his thinking had been dominated by Radcliffe Brown's somewhat anankastic preoccupation with kinship, lineages and formal social roles. My own special interests in anthropology were inspired by a rather un-British concern with personality development (a field which had been tentatively explored in the 1920's by Rivers, Seligman and Barrett, only to be outlawed by later social theorists as excessively subjective and impressionistic, surrendering the field to American pioneers such as Sapir, Ruth Benedict, Margaret Mead and Erik Erikson). Derek Freedman was sufficiently interested in personality, and I in the formal organization of society, for us to plan a joint expedition, in which we would each from our own point of view study a community of Iban tribespeople, living in a long-house village far in the interior of Sarawak. Freedman set out first, and did in fact complete a very thorough social and cultural analysis of this community; but my collaboration was thwarted by an outbreak of tribal violence, culminating in the murder of the Governor of Sarawak, which led to a temporary ban on the admission of any additional anthropologists. I had cause to be grateful in the end for this interruption of our plans, because my own field work was diverted, quite profitably, to my native country, India. In spite of this set-back, Derek Freedman's interest in the psychological dimensions of culture continued to grow. After some years he re-read Freud's and later neo-Freudians' interpretations of the unconscious significance of tribal rituals; then, wishing to employ Freudian insights in order to better understand patterns of relationships in the societies which he had studied, he underwent a personal analysis. At about the same time, he discovered the writings of ethologists such as Lorenz, Tinbergen, Hinde and Washburn. Some five years ago, while on sabbatical leave in London, he divided his time between the library of the Institute of

Psycho-analysis, the Regent's Park Zoo, and the offices of a popular tabloid, the Daily Mirror. In the zoo, he concentrated his observations on a few families of chimpanzees, studying their repertoire of gestures and facial expressions, and noting how the young seemed to respond instinctively from a very early age, not only to particular warning signals, gestures of threat, but also to an array of facial expressions. In the newspaper office, he collected several hundred examples of "candid camera" shots of people taken unawares, often at moments of anxiety, fear, anger or joy; he sought to single out, in these human instances, identifiable units of expression which could be compared with similar elements in primate behavior.

It is a commonplace of ethological observation that most gregarious species accept a leader of the herd, and often marshall their members into a simple or more complex status hierarchy. A very frequent example of "threat behavior" is an unblinking stare, before which the subordinate member flinches and yields ground; while the action of baring the teeth in a grin is a very common indicator of fear. The haughty stare, the deferential smile and the submissive crouch can all be found formalized in the etiquette of human hierarchial societies.

In human social intercourse, we tend to be preoccupied with consciously perceived cognitive messages; but at the same time we are often vaguely aware of communications of mood, which may even be quite at variance with what the other person is actually saying. On the literary plane, D. H. Lawrence was one of many who protested that our species' spectacular exploitation of its cognitive faculties, although richly rewarded in terms of technological mastery, has left the "feeling side" of our natures relatively impoverished and poorly developed; and in recent years, this complaint has been renewed by the Hippies, who reproach us Squares for only partly living. It is interesting to reflect that this movement, which we tend to dismiss as an emotional tantrum on the part of those who cannot make a success of their lives, may in fact be drawing attention to a very real frustration of a part of our psycho-biological endowment.

I find myself in danger of straying from my theme: but I should only like to say that having renewed contact with Derek Freedman recently, and ranged with him over the latest developments in human genetics, in ethology and in object-relations theory, I find myself looking forward eagerly to his next book, in which he draws upon his rich field observations in Sarawak and Samoa in order to show how all these disciplines can be integrated in a meaningful analysis of human social behavior.

I mentioned earlier in this paper that small isolated primitive societies have traditionally been the target for anthropologists' investigations; but this is no longer the case—partly, because isolated societies are becoming increasingly rare, so that field work perforce has to be concerned more and more with processes of rapid acculturalization, and less with the recording of once static social institutions, and partly because many workers in applied fields, such as social work, criminology, preventive medicine, epidemiology and social psychiatry have had their eyes opened to the existence of sub-cultures embedded within the large urban societies of the West. In many cases, the behavior of members of these subcultures can only be understood if we address ourselves to the same problems which are encountered by an anthropologist in the field, although not necessarily confining ourselves to his methods of inquiry.

For example, in my own psychiatric epidemiology research unit in Edinburgh, our preliminary surveys of the ecology of attempted suicide, crimes of violence, child neglect and petty delinquency all lead us to certain disadvantaged sections of the population; and yet we know that there are many families in these areas which show none of these forms of pathological behavior. Within these sub-communities, certain values are prevalent, certain models of anti-

social behavior are common: our current interest lies in
studying the acquisition, or repudiation, of values and behavior patterns which have become identified with these
social-problem areas.

Many years ago, Japanese ethologists carried out some
instructive experiments with troops of monkeys, by offering
them a mirror to play with, or a new and tasty food. They
noted that if young, immature monkeys took up the innovation it was disseminated only slowly through the group,
whereas if an adult male, high in the status hierarchy, did
so, then the spread was rapid. In our own present-day society, thanks to the glare of publicity in the mass media,
the very reverse seems to be the case: innovative patterns
initiated by the young and immature on one campus are
imitated by their age-mates on campuses all over the country, while their elders look on with apparently impotent
indignation.

In our research, we focus upon one aspect of behavior
at a time, and alternate between large-scale surveys, and
more intensive studies of small samples, as we seek the
causes of maladaptive phenomena. These limitations are
necessary if we are to make a small contribution to the
scientific study of social pathology.

At the same time, one cannot help looking up from one's
desk, from time to time, and noting with wonder the changes
which are sweeping over the whole world. If we were able
to leap forward a hundred, or two hundred years—always
with the hopeful proviso that global overkill has not been
let loose—it would not surprise me if this second half of the
20th century were seen as a turning point. This, after all,
is the epoch in which communications have suddenly become
world-wide and, thanks to Telstar, virtually instantaneous;
in which the material products of neo-industrial society are
spreading all over the globe, creating an unprecedented
world-wide uniformity in what anthropologists have been
wont to call the artifacts of human societies. In other words,

technological development is already forcing into being a single world community; and yet politically, every country lags behind. Hitherto, concepts of world-wide order have been phrased in terms of the victory of one particular set of values, be it Christendom or Islam, Capitalism or Communism: the idea of a world community which could incorporate and tolerate widely different sets of values still seems far off. Yet is this really true? Surely the occurrence of very similar manifestations of "student protest" all over the world has been a reminder that currents of thought now tend to be world-wide. In contrast, we find only very halting progress towards constructive co-operation; perhaps societies can move towards a greater blending and mutual acceptance, only when the great inequalities which separate the rich and the poor peoples have been lessened. This may well be the next great challenge facing human ingenuity—simply to give the assurance of food, health and education to the masses of mankind. Once these primary needs have been met, who knows what new developments we may see when human energies hitherto channeled into cognitive and materially productive activities are liberated and directed towards a fuller development of the affective and intuitive aspects of our being.

In the past, one society after another has evolved a privileged class, whose children were better fed, better educated and hence better equipped for intellectual exploration and discovery than the mass of their fellows, even in the countries which claim to be democracies. It is only in our own lifetimes that access to economic, social and cultural advancement has become widely spread. The early consequences, one must admit, have not been entirely encouraging; but this is the path on which our foot is set, and there can be no turning back.